Pat Teague and AJ CARR hit the BIG D-**they DELIVERED**! As a born again Naval Academy varsity football player and 2 time heavyweight boxing champ I knew I was an ambassador for Christ on the field or in the ring. I carried that ambition over to 24 years as a naval nuclear submarine captain as well as 15 years as a private and public sector IT director. However this book articulates how any person can be that ambassador by following the 7 D's. I sure could have used this game plan early on my service and avoided mistakes. Read it ! Use it! and you will **get it DONE** no matter where you are serving.
Captain Bruce W Cavey USN (ret) But not retired from serving

"I've known AJ and Pat for over 30 years and I cannot think of a better pair to co-author a book titled "Winning Ways for Life." If there has ever been two men that have lived a "winning life" it is AJ and Pat. I know I am challenged and encouraged by the stories and principles outlined in their book and I'm certain you will be, as well."
Johnny Evans
Eastern NC Director-FCA

"The principles in this book have helped prepare me for the battles in my life and are a constant source of practical wisdom for me to draw from. Each play really works and brings daily victory."
Morocco Brown - Assistant Director of Player Personnel for the Indianapolis Colts.

"He (Pat Teague) was one of best leaders and players I ever had the pleasure to coach, He was an example of what a student-athlete should be off the field as well as on the field. "He's an all-around, All-America guy. As good as he was in football; he's an even better person."
Coach Joe Pate – Former Defensive Coordinator and former Assoc. Athletic Director of NC State University

"When I sat down to talk to A.J., and this has been over 31 years, I always felt like I was not going to read something that was 180 degrees from what I said. As a coach, I had a great deal of respect that

A.J. wanted to get the story, he wanted to write the story, and he had in his mind that he wasn't going to jump away from it to be more controversial."
-- UNC basketball coach Roy Williams

"I consider him a great friend. When he had his hip replaced, I visited him in the Duke hospital. And so I have two hip replacements. We're kind of brothers in that regard. We kind of kid each other about setting alarms off together."
-- Duke basketball coach Mike Krzyzewski

"Most of us would settle for the kind of inscription that could easily be his epitaph: "Here lies the nicest, kindest man you could hope to meet. ... and a darn good sportswriter."
-- East Carolina athletics director Terry Holland

Pat and A.J. have been friends, mentors, and a great source of inspiration for me for years as a fellow brother-in-Christ. Winning Plays for Life encapsulates their decades of experience and God-given wisdom into an easy to read and apply guide to experiencing all that God has for anyone who would claim His Name, follow His Son, and seek to live by His Word. I'm so thankful that these two humble men of God took the time to share all that they have learned with me…and now, with you, too!
– Steve Noble - National Talk Show Host for Called2Action Radio & Rep for Harvest America Greg Laurie

Winning
PLAYS FOR
LIFE

FROM THE PERSPECTIVE OF A HALL OF FAME
SPORTSWRITER & FORMER ATHLETE

A.J. CARR & PAT TEAGUE

WESTBOW
PRESS®
A DIVISION OF THOMAS NELSON
& ZONDERVAN

WestBow Press books may be ordered through booksellers or by contacting:

WestBow Press
A Division of Thomas Nelson & Zondervan
1663 Liberty Drive
Bloomington, IN 47403
www.westbowpress.com
1 (866) 928-1240

ISBN: 978-1-5127-6417-8 (sc)
ISBN: 978-1-5127-6416-1 (e)

Library of Congress Control Number: 2016919101

Print information available on the last page.

WestBow Press rev. date: 10/02/2017

DEDICATION OF THIS BOOK

I dedicate this book to my beautiful bride, Sheila, the heartbeat of my heart, my best friend, and the awesome mother to our children. Thanks for being the very best teammate!

- To my children, Brianna, Ethan, and Rachel
- To my mom & dad, Happy & Dave; brothers Chris, Steve, Terry, and sister Bonnie
- To all my Teammates & Coaches—Thanks for being an extended Family!
- To my Crossroads Fellowship Church Family

ALL THE GLORY GOES TO MY HERO, JESUS! (Who is showing me the Way, the Truth & the Winning Plays for Life)

Pat Teague

I dedicate this book to Nancy, my wonderful wife and devoted mother to our sons Greg & Brad

- To their wives, Danette and Caroline
- To grandsons Huntley, James, Mason, William, and Baker.
- To my devout parents, Naomi Carr and Arminius Carr and loving sister Susan
- To the many coaches and athletes who have demonstrated the *Winning Plays*
- To all my "teammates" at the News & Observer who have been so helpful through all the years!

Most of all, to my Lord and Savior Jesus Christ— to Him be all the Glory.

A.J. Carr

CONTENTS

Introduction...ix

Chapter 1   Direction 1

Chapter 2   Determination 14

Chapter 3   Diligence 26

Chapter 4   Discipline 33

Chapter 5   Discernment 40

Chapter 6   Destiny...48

Chapter 7   The Diesel! – Grace - Power...55

Chapter 8   More Stories on the Winning Plays for Life 64

INTRODUCTION

—A .J. CARR

Having sweated profusely over sports stories that usually totaled 500 to 1,000 words for more than fifty years, contributing to a book sounded overwhelming.

A book? When I often struggled to find a lead paragraph for an eighteen-inch article.

But Long-time and persuasive friend Pat Teague, a former football star who ministers in the Raleigh, NC, area, submitted a theme and suggested teaming up on a book during a conversation at the Finley YMCA in Raleigh, N.C.

Having known Pat since his glory days at NC State in the 1980s and aware of his deep faith, I agreed to join him on this endeavor. With much prayer and reliance on the Lord, we focused on what Pat titled *Winning Plays for Life.*

My role and hope was to find a way to weave a few athletic examples into this devotional publication bearing a strong Christian emphasis.

The list below, which will be explored in more detail later, is a snapshot of important keys to achieving a high level of living spiritually and practically.

Winning Plays for Life:
* Direction
* Determination
* Diligence
* Discipline
* Discernment
* Destination
* Diesel

In his progression as an athlete, a devoted husband and father, professional engineer, and minister, Pat has long practiced what he has preached. He was a stellar three sports standout at Raleigh's Sanderson High School and football star at NC State, where he set the school single-game record with 26 official tackles in the 1986 Peach Bowl verses Virginia Tech and 29 unofficial stops against North Carolina. Later he played in the NFL before returning to Raleigh after injuries short-circuited his career.

It was special for Wolfpack fans to watch Pat play. It has been more rewarding to interview him, when he would share his faith and give glory to God.

As the following pages illustrate, application of Pat's "Winning Plays For Life," supporting Bible verses and questions can be helpful in virtually every area of a person's life: Faith, family, profession, sports, and most any other endeavor. I pray this book will be spiritually enriching and that it will lift all of us to a more devoted, fulfilling Christian life and toward the ultimate destination, Heaven. To God be the glory.

—PAT TEAGUE

You are always one play away from a big play. Would you like to know the secret of going from good to great? Or would you like to learn how to prepare for your moment in the sun, and to learn how to position yourself for the "big plays?" Do you want to make an impact on this world?

Using sports history of victories and defeats, this book is about getting you ready for the moment that can be the game changer, the "big play" in your life or someone else's, or even literally in a game of competition. These winning plays transcend the athletic arena and can be used in any arena of life. The plays and principles we reveal here have played out repeatedly in the lives of numerous people in many different kinds of arenas in life and in sport.

Since the focus of the book is on the athletic arena, we present our points through examples and interviews with athletes through the eyes of a Hall of Fame sports writer, A. J. Carr. As an athlete, I discovered these "plays" in a relentless pursuit of the universal truths that would give me the edge I needed to beat my opponent or myself. Many athletes have achieved more than I have, but what I discovered in my pursuit of championships with my teammates and endless hours of praying, practicing, dreaming, sweating, bleeding, and training were principles I could apply to any area of my life. I treasure the experiences with all my teammates and coaches through the years.

This book is not about my achievements or a desire to relive my "glory days," nor is it about A. J.'s wonderful ability to capture the true stories of athletes and athletic achievement. It is an attempt to pass on what we have learned to help you reach your destiny in life. I like to call destiny your "sweet spot," the place where you are doing what you were created to do, making the most effective impact on your community and glorifying God through your life.

What is "glorifying God?" First Corinthians 10:31 "... *whatever you do, do all to the glory of God.*" This is reflecting some aspect of God's character through your actions, achievements or habits.

The athletes and events mentioned in this book are taken from the accounts of Hall of Fame sports writer, A. J. Carr, who observed, recorded, and reported accurately what he witnessed. When A.J. interviewed me during my athletic career, I could always count on him to get the story right. He is a true journalist! He did not add his opinion or agenda to the events or people he interviewed. I believe God has given him the ability to see, listen, and communicate what really took place, rather than what he thought took place. A.J.'s humble demeanor always demanded my highest respect, and through the years we have developed a genuine friendship that I treasure. A.J. has been running the winning plays in his own life for over 70 years as a Brother in Christ, Husband, Father, Friend and Sports Writer.

The purpose of the *Winning Plays for Life: From the Perspectives of a Hall of Fame Sports Writer and a Former Athlete"* is to help you run a winning race through life by being prepared to make the most of your opportunities.

When the apostle Paul wrote in 1 Corinthians 9:24 NASB, *"Run in such a way that you may win,"* he emphasized that our lives are like races that have beginnings, ends, and lasting results. There is even a crowd, "so great a cloud of witnesses" (Heb. 12:1) spiritually cheering us on. Why are they cheering? What are they looking for? To see how well you make the most of your moment to make the game-winning play.

Competing in this race at a winning level is a process, not a single event. It takes a certain level of maturity to compete at a winning level. What does it mean to be a mature man or woman, and what does it take to become one?

You may have grown physically into a man or woman, but have you grown emotionally (in the soul)? Have you grown spiritually? I confess that there are times when I whine and complain because I don't get what I want when I want it. This is a good indication that I still have a lot of growing up to do.

I shared these seven principles or "winning plays" with A. J. when he described his desire to write a book that was not just about his interviews over 50-plus year period, but about what he can pass on about winning in life. As we tested these principles or "plays"—direction, determination, diligence, discipline, discernment, destiny, and the "diesel" (power)—against his experiences with all the athletes he interviewed and the many sporting events he reported on, we realized we had the makings of great book. The seven plays can be described in a single sentence…

If you daily choose to Diligently practice your Disciplines with Determination in God's divine Direction and power (Diesel) using Discernment, then you will have a great Destiny.

When it all comes together it is like a baseball player hitting a home run in the bottom of the 9th inning, a running back breaking free to score the winning touchdown, a basketball player making the winning shot at the buzzer, or a surfer who catches the ultimate wave! Let's unpack this statement containing the "seven Ds," which took a lifetime of triumphs and failures to learn, because if you run these plays on a daily basis you have the potential to break loose and score big in the race of life. Get ready for a great experience!

Chapter 1

DIRECTION

"Turn right." —TomTom (GPS)

"Trust in the Lord with all your heart and do not lean on your own understanding. In all your ways acknowledge Him, and He will direct your path straight" (Prov. 3:5–6) NASB

Marcus Hilliard's father was gone. His mother was dead.

Enter football coach David Cutcliffe and his wife, Karen, who opened their hearts and home to the young boy and made him part of their family, which already included three children.

The Cutcliffes are white. Marcus is black. Color did not matter.

It happened in Oxford, Mississippi, when Cutcliffe, who had been a renowned offensive coach and quarterback guru at Tennessee, was rebuilding and elevating the Ole Miss football program to championship status. Since then he has transformed once downtrodden Duke into a winner and restored some of the past gridiron glory.

But back to Marcus. He was a friendly youth, polite and one of the first students to welcome Cutcliffe's son, Chris, when he enrolled at the Oxford school as a sixth-grader. The two boys quickly bonded, played together, and hung out often at the Cutcliffe house.

When Marcus was in the eighth grade, his world got rocked again. His loving, caring mother died of cancer. While battling grief and uncertainty, he moved around, living with various family members. The nomadic arrangement didn't work out. Sometimes the environment was dangerous.

Perceptive Karen was aware and told her husband one day that Marcus was moving in with them. Coach Cutcliffe welcomed him with paternalistic warmth. The Cutcliffes became Marcus' "Mom" and "Dad," and Marcus became a son and brother in their home.

They gave Marcus renewed hope and security, provided for him just as they did their other three children and enabled him to get a college education at the University of Tennessee. Ever grateful, Marcus later worked in Duke's athletics department and is cognizant his good, stable life no doubt would be much different if not for the direction and love a Christian coach and his family provided.

The Cutcliffes' lives also have been enriched. They got another son.

—A.J. Carr

—Pat Teague

What is "direction"? The Cutcliffes followed God's lead to help Marcus find direction at a critical time in his life. As players need timely instruction from their coach, we also need instruction in which direction we must take in our daily lives and our future because ***the decisions you make today can determine your destiny tomorrow.***

First, we must select the right team and the right coach. Who better to coach you than the Divine Designer to give you direction? Direction comes only through Jesus Christ, the ultimate life coach, who shows us the way and tells us the truth so we can have true, abundant life (John 14:6). When I go to Jesus first, I initially receive a peace to my soul so I can clearly see ahead. To see your reflection in water, it must be calm. In the same way, Jesus brings peace/calm to my soul when I go to Him first and the Holy Spirit is able to reveal the next step.

Using another sports illustration, if I make Jesus the "head coach" of my life instead of one of many advisors then I simplify my life and decision-making. The direction He gives may lead me to get wise counsel from a trustworthy mentor or a book or a trusted friend or my bible study group. The team He coaches does not lose because Jesus conquered hell and death through the cross and resurrection. "Thanks be to God who always leads us in His triumph, so that we may manifest the sweet aroma of Christ" (2 Corinthians 2:14).

The key to victory is to make it about Him and His team. When it is all about you, that sweet aroma turns rancid. A great example is Vernon Davis, a first-round draft pick by the 49ers in 2006, the highest paid tight end in the NFL. When it was all about him in his first three seasons, his contribution to the team was disappointing (265, 589, and 358 yards respectively, and just 2 touchdowns). Coach Mike Singletary made him leave the field after an incident against Seattle and told him he was an embarrassment to his team and the city of San Francisco. Singletary told Davis that he could be great if he would play for the team, not for himself, and Davis told sports writer Bill Reiter that he made a decision that day to put himself aside: "I … remember [Singletary] saying, 'Vernon, when you put the team first, then you'll start to take off.' So, I did that. Since then, life has been really good." Vernon continued, "I changed my life around and I became more of a leader, because in the beginning it was all about me and that's not right. You don't want it to be all about you. I find it that, when it's more about the team and you put the team first, you have more success."

What a great decision! Davis's numbers took off. In the 2009 season, he had 965 receiving yards and 13 touchdowns. In the 2010 and 2011 seasons, he had 914 and 792 receiving yards, respectively. The lesson from Davis's career is not to make life all about "me", but to turn our attention to God's team and His winning game plan. This is also a good description of humility, which is about "we," not "me."

Another great example of a man having direction is Chris Spielman, an All-American linebacker from Ohio State University and an All-Pro linebacker for the Detroit Lions and Buffalo Bills. With 1,138 tackles, he is the all-time tackle leader for the Lions, and he is a member of the College Football Hall of Fame. When his wife, Stefanie, became ill with cancer, he retired from football and shaved his head when she lost her hair. I met him at an NC State football practice, where we had a great conversation about what really matters in life. My respect grew because of his devotion to his family. He was a great football player, but more importantly, he is a great man. Stefanie died in 2009 after another bout with cancer, but Chris continues to fight against cancer with the Stefanie Spielman Fund for Breast Cancer Research. Chris is now a Sports Broadcaster for ESPN.

When I was a teenager, I earned some respect with the older guys on the athletic field, so they began to invite me to their parties. In the summer between my eighth- and ninth-grade years, I became aware of what direction these parties could take me. I had broken up with my girlfriend of two weeks, and I was ready for a party. However, once I was at the party I noticed a teammate coming out of the bathroom with his hair wet and matted from a feeble attempt to rinse vomit out. Another teammate was arguing with a girl. I heard a small, still voice ask, *Is this what you want out of life? Give me a chance and trust me with everything.* I left the party and never looked back. I went home and opened my Living Bible translation, and the pages fell open to "Do you want favor with God and man?" (Prov. 3:4). I said to myself, *Yes! I want to be cool with God and my peers.* Then I read, "Then do not let good judgment and common sense leave you. Trust me with everything and do not trust yourself" (Prov. 3:5). I surrendered my will to submit to His will, and I made Jesus the head coach of my life. I immediately felt a sense of relief and peace. The decision I made that day determined my eternal destiny!

I had a praying Mom, sweet Happy, who rejoiced over my decision to make Jesus my "Head Coach" for life! I had told her as a young boy I wanted to play on "God's Team". She rejoiced when I finally joined! There is always someone praying for you! I was so blessed to have her constantly interceding for my siblings and me. During the games I played in, my mom would be praying fervently in the stands with a Scripture Promises book in her hands hardly watching the game. My family has been a source of strength and inspiration to me. My brothers and sister are inspiring to me in their pursuits to be the best they can be. My Dad was a faithful, hardworking man who supported me until his untimely death on the morning after I reported to football camp my second year in college. I miss my Dad and the way he laughed.

"There's a way that seems right to man ..." (Prov. 16:25).

Remember, you need instruction in the direction you must take in your daily life because **the decisions you make today determine your destiny tomorrow.**

Pat Morley, who lost $38 million in one day, wrote, "You could climb the ladder of success and find out the ladder is leaning on the wrong building." What a moment of regret and remorse! You must first get God's divine direction, which comes only through Jesus Christ, the ultimate Life Coach, who shows us the way and tells us the truth so we can have true abundant life (John 14:6).

We can be fooled by our own five senses (Prov. 16:25). I can be deceived by following my heart when it is not directed by the Holy Spirit. Disney has it wrong—if we follow our hearts just to be happy, we will never be satisfied or at peace. When you look inside your heart without God, you find three things that will try to govern your decision making--your appetites, your emotional needs, or your own ego or self-importance (which all result into a selfish, lonely, and empty existence).

Our opponent, satan, uses three plays to stop us from scoring in life. Satan is the expert at disguising his blitz calls on us. He uses the lust of the flesh, our appetites; the lust of the eyes, our pleasures; and the boastful pride of life, our egos (1 John 2:15–17). These wage war against the Spirit because they encourage us to pursue instant gratification, not our purpose (Gal. 5:16–18). In other words, we can be led down a deceptive path that seems right if we go on only what we think, what we feel, or what we want. In John 10:10, Jesus reveals Satan's plays as "steal," "kill," and "destroy." Jesus tells you and me what His playbook will produce--He came to give us life until it overflows abundantly! The kingdom of heaven is described in Romans 4:17 as righteousness, peace, and joy in the Holy Spirit. These results are the exact opposite of Satan's goals. We are confronted every day with the choice of which coach we will listen to. God tells us what His plays are in Micah 6:8: "to do justice (righteousness), to love kindness (leads to peace), and to walk humbly with your God (results in joyful fellowship with the Holy Spirit). True success in this life is when we have righteousness, peace, and joy produced from the effort we put into your area of expertise. John Wooden said it this way, "Success is peace of mind which is a direct result of self-satisfaction in knowing you did your best to become the best you are capable of becoming."

If we present ourselves to God as willing teammates (Rom. 12:1–2), then we can be coached to hear what God thinks, feels, and wants. If we want to know God's will for our lives, we must surrender our will to listen to instruction and eternal wisdom. Be coachable: if you want to receive true direction, do not be afraid of candid instruction. *If you truly want direction you must be willing to receive correction.*

God will satisfy our every righteous desire, or He would not have given them to us. However, there is a time and place for them to be realized and enjoyed (Ps. 145:16, 19).

For example, if you are a man, your sexual appetite is to be satisfied with your wife, not by every woman you meet. If you are a single man, wait for her. She is worth waiting for! Rely upon His great game plan to fulfill you completely in His timing (Jer. 29:11–13). First, decide to trust God with all your heart; do not lean on your own heart and understanding, but acknowledge Him in all ways, and He will direct your path (Prov. 3:5–6).

Jesus came to give us abundantly overflowing life. Once we have that, our bearings are set and our destinations are sure. It is only then that we will be equipped with His Spirit to face the fears, the pain, and the challenges of life. Thus, we earn the respect to be positive influences in the world, the beginning of true manhood or womanhood.

Now, when we seek direction in athletics, academics, our professional careers, partnerships, or relationships, we have the world's best Guidance Counselor to define our goals. He will make known to us the path of life (Ps. 16:11).

I have come to realize that there is not a bench in the game of life. I am always on the field of play, but I can choose not to participate, to sit on the field. However, when I do this, I am in the way of those who are actively playing the game.

I have huddles—prayer—so I can get the plays, but I do not spend all my time there, or a delay-of-game penalty will be called.

You may not have realized this until now, but you have been heavily recruited by God to play on His team. Your skills are unique for playing the position that He wants you to play. My teammates and I need you on this team, playing the position only you can play. We cannot play the position you have been divinely designed to play.

Not even the greatest Christians can play the position you have been divinely designed to play. His thoughts about you outnumber the sand on the beach, and you are fearfully and wonderfully made (Ps. 139). You have been packaged by God for greatness, so allow Him to develop all He put inside you fully. You are a highly sought-after recruit to play the unique position that has been divinely designed by our Creator. It is never too late for you to start playing your position in life.

When Vince Lombardi was 43, he was still a position coach at a small university. He did not become the head coach of the Green Bay Packers until he was 46. Now his name is on the Super Bowl trophy. In the Bible, Caleb was 85 years old when he conquered the land promised to him (Josh. 14:6–15, 15:14). You are never too young or too old! A young boy offered his lunch of five loaves and two fish to Jesus in order to feed a multitude (John 6:1–15). Daniel and three of his friends were teenagers when they impacted an entire kingdom (Daniel 1–5).

We can play on a lonely team that consists only of ourselves if our sins separate us from joining His team. It is like we received the ultimate penalty that gets us thrown out of the game. The wages of this sin is death, eternal separation from God, and loved ones (Rom. 6:23).

That is why Jesus had to sacrifice Himself--to get you back in the game. God demonstrated His love for us when Christ died on the cross to pay the penalty for us when we were sinners and ejected from the game.

Here's what we need to do to get in the game of life:

Surrender our lives to Jesus—He will show us *the way* the game is played. He will tell us the *truth*, and He has given us the Bible as the playbook. He liberates us from our sins to give us a new *life* (John 14:6). This is the most crucial step in deciding to trust God with all our hearts.

How do we surrender? We don't lean on our own hearts and understanding but acknowledge Him in all our ways, and He will direct our paths (Prov. 3:5–6). Jesus came to give us abundantly overflowing life!

Here is what we need to do:

1. Admit we have sinned. If we confess our sins, Jesus is faithful in forgiving us for all our mistakes and shortcomings (1 John 1:9).

2. Ask Jesus to lead and direct our lives. If we confess with our mouths that Jesus *is* Lord and believe in our hearts that God raised Him from the dead, we will be saved and rescued from the guilt of our sins (Rom. 10:9).

3. Repent—decide not to go our own ways but decide to follow Jesus in His way. He came to give us abundant life (Isaiah 1:18, Acts 2:38).

4. Thank Jesus daily for loving, saving, delivering, and accepting us. Thank Jesus by the way you live (Col. 3:17).

5. Stand up and look up for ways to participate in life. There are many needs in this world. Let's open our eyes and follow the Holy Spirit's lead (John 14:26).

6. Start with family and friends. Be a part of their lives. Be a team player. Life is not only about you and what you want, feel, or think. Life is about what God thinks, feels, and wants. Let Jesus transform you into a team player (Rom. 12:1–2).

7. Begin to participate on a team with others who have a relationship with Jesus. In other words, get involved in a local church that believes Jesus is the way, the truth, and the life—and believes in the Bible as your playbook for life. Also, get involved at your school or in your community with a ministry that encourages you to be your best. For example, the Fellowship of Christian Athletes (FCA) was a great outlet for me to grow into the man I wanted to be and to find friends with similar goals. I am so thankful for this ministry that enriched my high school and college days! Later on in my life, Crossroads Fellowship's Doug Gamble and I teamed up to launch Sports Missions Outreach (SMO), a ministry to help you run a winning race for life through Christ.

Once you have done these seven things, your bearings are set and your destination is sure.

Now you are in the game, and you can watch Jesus make big plays in you and through you.

Praise God for your decision to join His undefeated team. Welcome to the team! Now that you have scored the ultimate touchdown/goal/winning shot, It's time to celebrate! Football players like to spike the ball and do a dance to celebrate. Go and tell someone. Celebrate! Please do not neglect doing this.

God even gives you a uniform, equipment to wear—the armor of God (Eph. 6:10–18), and a playbook. Our playbook, the Bible, is filled with plays to run that have the potential to be big scoring plays each time they are executed.

Now, when we seek direction in athletics, academics, professional career, partnerships, or relationships, we have the world's best guidance counselor to help us define our goals (Ps. 16:11).

Take-Aways: Direction

Definition: A bearing, line, or course along which a person moves.

Fruit: Peace of mind, clarity, perspective, focus.

1. Jesus is the Way-maker "You will make known to me the path of life; In Your presence is fullness of joy; In Your right hand there are pleasures forever". (Ps.16:11)

   "And your ears will hear a word behind you, 'This is the way; walk in it' whenever you turn to the right or to the left" (Is. 30:21), (John 14:6).NASB

2. Decisions you make today determine your destiny tomorrow.

3. You have been created for a purpose and packaged for greatness. (Ps. 139).

4. Listen to those who have gone before you and who have done it right (Prov. 15:22).

   Be coachable. If you want to receive true direction, do not be afraid of candid instruction.

5. Face the fears, the pain, and the challenges that earn you the respect you need to be a positive influence. (Josh. 1:1–10).

6. Satan uses three defensive plays against you, and Jesus has three offensive plays to defeat them. Satan's plays: to kill, to steal, to destroy (lust of the flesh); lust of the eyes (need for entertainment), boastful pride (ego) (John 10:10, 1 John 2:15–17). Jesus' plays: righteousness, peace, and joy (the way to do justice); the truth (love and kindness); the life (to walk humbly with God) (Micah 6:6–8, Rom. 14:17, John 14:6).

7. If we trust God with everything, then Jesus will entrust us with everything pertaining to life and godliness (Matt. 16:25, Ps. 145:16–19, 2 Peter 1:3-4).

Additional Scriptures: Jer. 29:11–13, Prov. 3:5–6, Gal. 5:16–18.

If you daily choose to Diligently practice your Disciplines with Determination in God's divine Direction and power (Diesel) using Discernment, then you will have a great Destiny.

Let's Talk about Direction

1. Have you allowed Jesus to give you direction as the Head Coach of your life, or is He just an advisor?

2. Read Proverbs 14:12 and Proverbs 16:25. What do they mean to you? What can get you on the wrong track?

3. Read Jeremiah 29:11 and Proverbs 3:5–6. How do you get God's direction for your life?

4. What are your goals in life, spiritually, mentally, and physically?

5. What do you want out of life?

6. Where do you think you are going in life?

Chapter 2

DETERMINATION

"Don't give up. Don't you ever give up."
—Jim Valvano

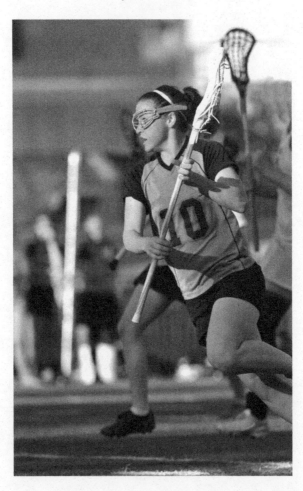

In many respects, Kyle Maynard was a lot like his peers.

As a kid, he roughed it up in street hockey and played on the defensive line for his sixth grade football team. As a teenager he enjoyed video games, excelled as a student, and wrestled for his Suwanee (Ga.) Collins High School team.

Not bad, especially for someone born with congenital amputation. He has no hands. His arms are small and stubby, ending at elbow length. His legs are slender and short, stopping where most people have knee caps.

But Maynard sought no sympathy. His will is tough as barbed wire, his heart bigger than a wrestling mat, his faith strong.

"Nothing is Impossible with God," he said at a prep wrestling match in 2003, drawing on a Bible verse --Luke 1:37.

During a high school tournament in Chapel Hill, N.C., Maynard caught your eye before he stepped on the mat. Although he lost numerous times early in his career, the resilient kid didn't lose heart or his competitive spirit. With steely determination he won 36 matches his senior year at Collins High.

He attacked and tied opponents into a pretzel-like position with his short arms, short legs and a chin lock. Once in his grip, it was like being trapped in a vise. Maynard also won a World's Strongest Teen title in Atlanta, bench-pressing 240 pounds 23 times.

Since those youthful days Maynard, now a grown man, has gone to college and reached more unimaginable heights. In 2012, he climbed Mount Kilimanjaro by crawling 19,340 feet in a grueling 10-day span, and became the first quadruple amputee to accomplish that feat without assistance.

There's more. He has competed in martial arts, won 2 ESPY awards, been enshrined in the National Wrestling Hall of Fame, written "No Excuses," a book that made the New York Times Best Seller list. He became a motivational speaker and CrossFit Gym owner.

As Maynard said, "Nothing is impossible for God."

—A.J. Carr

"The Lion ... does not retreat before any" (Prov. 30:30).

—PAT TEAGUE

When NHL hockey legend Glen Wesley was asked which attribute is most important for success (passion, skill, talent, or determination) he answered, "Determination. If you [also] have the other three attributes, there is no bar. The sky's the limit."

We must be determined to stay the course, no matter what comes. The lion, which is mightiest among beasts, instinctively knows this and retreats before no one. Without determination, we will easily give up when adversity comes. The temptation to give up will overwhelm us because we did not make up our mind before the game began. Determination begins with commitment, so a commitment to the direction that sets your course is vital.

Challenges will arise. You can count on it! Adversity can purify our motives and direction because it causes us to consider the cost of what we are doing and to evaluate honestly, whether the pain to get there is worth it. "Blessed is the man who perseveres under trial. Once he has been approved he will receive the crown of life" (James 1:12) NASB.

How did Daniel in the Bible survive the invasion of his country, the loss of his parents and home, the stealing of his future and dreams, and enslavement? How did he become a major influence to four different kings and impact a secular hedonistic culture? The secret lies in Daniel 1:8, "But Daniel *made up his mind* that he would not defile himself ..." As a teenager, he made a decision to follow God's way of doing things no matter what! **He made up his mind!** Daniel loved God's presence in his everyday world more than life itself. Then God gave him favor, supernatural protection, three great friends from home, promotion, and enormous respect among the people. God was glorified throughout the country that enslaved him. God even revealed to him the future of all mankind. His life continues to influence and inspire us because he was determined to follow God. The purity of your direction determines the strength of your resolve.

(Read the book of Daniel in the Bible)

A burning drive to win can be a positive force and an expression of gratitude to your teammates and coaches. Your determined efforts and performance as a show of appreciation generates enthusiasm, which can be contagious to those around you and challenge them to overcome their own obstacles. A great player challenges his teammates to "up" their games. Some great players who have done this for their teams are Michael Jordan, Peyton Manning and Tim Duncan.

Michael Jordan's intensity and competitiveness was contagious to his teammates. Peyton Manning's drive for perfection and preparation caused his teammates to step up their level of preparation. Tim Duncan's unselfishness and consistency created unified championship teams year-end and year out.

Mental toughness is necessary if we are determined to stay committed to our goal. For example, throughout his career, Kobe Bryant has displayed mental toughness by playing injured. In the 2012 NBA All-Star game, he collided with Dwayne Wade, breaking his nose and suffering a concussion. In the next game, he came out on the court with a plastic mask and scored 32 points in 31 minutes for a victory over the Minnesota Timberwolves. Challenges always arise when we are attempting to become better at what we do (1 Peter 1:13–16), so do not be surprised by the obstacles or think you are the only one dealing with them. What is the difference in being an ordinary and an extraordinary player? It is giving that "extra" effort to improve, or that little extra to study, or that little extra after practice.

I encountered injuries, setbacks, opposition, and bad performances in my pursuit of being the best I could be in football. One of those setbacks became a defining moment in my life.

In the spring of my senior year at N.C. State, a third new coaching staff (3rd staff in during my 5 years there) had come to turn the football program around. At the time, I was recovering from a devastating injury. I had suffered a life-threatening allergic reaction during a game the previous season that had taken a tremendous toll on my body. Neither this new coaching staff nor I realized that my body was still recovering from that event. As a result, in spring drills I was not playing like a leader of the defense. I did not make a good impression, so I decided to fill my summer with two-a-day workouts to get my body back to NCAA Division I caliber football and focus my attention on God's promises from the Bible for my life. I decided to put myself through a disciplined routine. The new coaching staff still had me starting at the beginning of fall camp since I had been the starting linebacker and signal-caller for the past three years. However, after one scrimmage, they moved me to fourth string! I was crushed! Seeing my discouragement, my roommate, Scott Auer, gave me Proverbs 30:30, "The Lion … does not retreat before any". I appreciate God's gift of true friends who are there to "spot" you when you have to lift a heavy load. I was blessed to play on a team of players who had become close through all of our adversity.

I was given a choice that day: I could either give up and run away from the challenge or believe in God's promises for my life. I had to face the reality of what had happened. Looking back, this defining moment for me determined the difference between reaching true manhood and becoming a victim crippled with excuses. One more time, through my tears and my broken heart, I embraced the promise that, "No weapon formed against me will prosper; every tongue that accuses you in judgment you will condemn. This is the heritage of the servants of the LORD, and their vindication is from Me" (Is. 54:17). He gave me His "Gracerade" (will be discussed in later in the book) to rejuvenate my spirit and my inner man and give me the strength to show my face at the next practice. In my soul, where my emotions were raging, I had to get up from that devastating blow and keep fighting the good fight of faith. I had to face the pain and not run.

The all capital letters of "LORD" in Isaiah 54:17 meant that the covenant-keeping God was standing with me in this valley of disappointment and despair. This passage of Scripture helped me to recall what I had done all summer. I had gone to bed with my earphones on, listening to verses and inspirational songs. I woke up early and lifted my hands to heaven to praise and thank Him for another opportunity to see Him turn things around. This time of praise and thanksgiving fueled me with His grace *("Gracerade")* and the power to overcome. Then I went to work out before my job started. On my way home from work I fit in another workout to rebuild my body. I had my own version of two-a-day practices. On the weekends, I would visit friends and go to church. My mom was my nutritionist, helping to ensure I was on track—she was way ahead of her time. I put myself through a disciplined routine.

During my time on the fourth string, I had to choose every day to practice the disciplines of a starting linebacker with determination. My position coach could see it happening, so when an opportunity arose to get back in the lineup, he convinced the defensive coordinator to put me in. The rest is history, and I saw God rise in me. He put His "super" on my natural! God is supernatural! I can! You can! We can do all things through Christ's strength. (Phil. 4:13)

At the end of the year, I received what I consider the highest honor a player could receive from his peers; my teammates voted me their captain. I also received the Courageous Award and the Sportsmanship/ Integrity Award. I finished the year with the most tackles on the team, was on the list of the Top Ten for most tackles in school history at that time, and had the single-game record for tackles (26 official tackles in the Peach Bowl against Virginia Tech and 29 unofficial tackles—29 according to NCSU defensive coaching staff in the UNC game that year. The UNC total is under dispute because of a mix-up in record-keeping.) I was also selected to be on the first team All-ACC and was an honorable-mention All-American. I witnessed first-hand God's intervention and how personal He is to us. To God be the glory for all that occurred that season! The SETBACK became a SET UP to see God work in my life! How about you? Are you facing adversity or some setbacks? What is your decision going to be?

Clearly, we must courageously and soberly confront our mistakes or we will never correct them. If we ignore them or blame them on our teammates, we will be doomed to repeat them because we chose not to take responsibility for our own actions and decisions. You cannot correct what you do not confront. Failure to confront your mistakes is your selfish pride getting in the way of your success. Humble yourself to receive the instruction and correction you need so you can stay on course (1 Peter 5:5–10). To humble ourselves means to admit that God's way is always the best way to handle a situation. We must choose to surrender our will only to Jesus, not to our emotions, circumstances, or challenges. If we do, He will become our refuge and an endless source of encouragement, comfort, and strength in times of need (Heb. 4:15–16). When we allow God to instruct us, we can resist the opponent and stand firm in our faith (James 4: 6–8). Then, when we are knocked down, we can get back up and try again, and again and again, until we achieve the victory.

Dan Miller never made it to the NFL or the NBA but he accomplished his dreams in the midst of great obstacles. As a star basketball player at the age of 18, Dan set goals to become a pilot, a Physical Education Teacher, and a leader of his own band. However, he became ill. He thought it was a seasonal flu but it turned out to be Polio. Dan became completely paralyzed and needed help to even roll over in bed, but friends began to pray and God raised him off that bed. The effects on his physical body were substantial, but not on his spirit to live out his dreams. Dan survived, but Polio had taken a toll on his body. He lost 80% use of his legs; his right arm was paralyzed, except for two fingers and a limp thumb; and he had only 50% use of his left arm. In his words, he had to surround himself with dream makers not dream breakers. Dan determined he would shoot a basketball again so after three weeks of trying he made his first shot. Dan went on to practice so that he made 96 out of 100 free throws. He then learned how to play the guitar and formed a band to help pay for his Physical Education degree in college. Dan became a Physical Education Teacher who could not jump or run. Finally, he worked to get his pilot's license and now flies anywhere he wants to go. God put His SUPER on Dan's natural. Dan put in extra to become extra-ordinary.

Dan made a decision to continue to pursue his dream despite the obstacles. He decided not to allow his suffering to become an excuse to quit. What if he had decided to give up?

We can stunt our progress by making bad decisions. If you do not courageously confront your mistakes, you will never correct them. When you ignore your lapses in judgment or blame them on your teammates, you are doomed to repeat them. If you do not take responsibility for your actions, selfish pride will get in the way of your success. Therefore, humble yourself and be willing to accept coaching and correction so you can make the adjustments you need to keep on course. Tough times can refine you, purify your motives, and strengthen your resolve. The direction we have divinely received can purely burn bright and strong to fuel our passion to keep going when we are weary. ***Purity of purpose determines the strength of our resolve.***

Another way we can stunt our progress is by allowing the bitterness of others to infect us. We must not allow bitterness to infect our view of life because of the shortsighted views of others relating to our race, where we come from, our size, etc. One of my all-time favorite athletes, Jim Thorpe, a Native American, did not let others limit his potential. He is one the most diverse athletes of all time. He was a professional football, basketball, and baseball player, as well as a track decathlon star. Jim even won a dance contest! In the 1912 Olympics, someone stole his track shoes to discourage him. Undeterred, Jim found two mismatched track shoes of different sizes in the trash to make a pair. One shoe was larger than the other was so he had to wear an extra sock on one foot. Jim overcame the injustice and competed to win two gold medals! Jim Thorpe would not be denied! Determination in action! You cannot make everyone behave by your core values, but you can overcome their immaturity by forgiving them and staying focused on your God inspired direction. You cannot transform unless you transcend your differences. (Romans 12:1-2) Forgiveness is the key to transformation—from bitter to better. Bitterness is a disease that defiles many and causes trouble. (Hebrews 12:14-15) However, forgiveness brings peace and freedom.

Jesus knows all about injustice! He was betrayed by one his disciples (Judas) and was then framed with false witnesses. Jesus was abandoned by all of his close friends and loved ones—rejected by His community when they selected a known criminal to be set free instead Him. Jesus, the Nazarene, was a victim of prejudice and jealousy by the religious community, the Sanhedrin. He was beaten and whipped by the police of that time, the Roman guards. Jesus was murdered for political reasons, (Matthew 26-27) BUT He chose to forgive and stayed focused on His God inspired direction and purpose. Therefore, Jesus defeated the real enemy behind all the hatred and bigotry—satan. Jesus showed unconditional love towards those who were being blindly manipulated by the devil's deceitful ways. If we follow in Jesus' steps, we will not waste our time and efforts in the wrong direction, but instead will fulfill our destiny. He said to the heavenly Father, "Forgive them for they do not know what they are doing." (Luke 23:34) Jesus accomplished His purpose and brought us all the opportunity for true freedom.

Now that we have removed bad decisions and bitterness let us make our drive to win be a positive force with which we thank Jesus for His personal sacrifice that makes our personal victory possible (Col. 3:17, 23). He has our back even when no one else does, so we can completely unleash all of our resources to accomplish our goals. Because our enthusiasm can be contagious to those around us and challenge them to overcome their obstacles, our team will improve because each individual is determined to play their parts well.

National Hall of Fame wrestling coach, Bill Lam of UNC, has said that the first period in wrestling is all about the talent and skill of the wrestler. The second period is about which wrestler has put in the work and paid the price. The third period is about the wrestler who has the most heart or who wants it more. That wrestler with the heart and determination will be the winner of the match.

Jim Valvano, former head basketball coach for NC State and the 1983 NCAA National Championship "team of destiny" said it best when he was battling cancer, "Don't give up. Don't you ever give up!"

Valvano was inspiring to the nation and to all those were fighting similar battles. The 1983 NC State team that he coached is also a great example of determination and preventing doubts from paralyzing them. The experts predicted that each team they faced in the NCAA tournament would beat them, but the team was determined, and because of so many heart-stopping victories, they were known as the "Cardiac Pack." In the final game against the highly favored University of Houston, with only a second on the clock, Derek Whittenburg threw almost a half-court shot. As the ball fell short of the goal, Lorenzo Charles caught the ball and dunked it for the winning basket as time expired. Their opponents, including tournament's MVP Hakeem Olajuwon, were frozen in shock as the final buzzer sounded. The team's iron will to win was a reflection of the resilient spirit of their coach, who inspired them and the nation.

Doug Flutie, the Boston College quarterback who threw the most famous "Hail Mary" pass in NCAA history to beat the University of Miami with no time left on the game clock, is an amazing example of determination! He played 21 years of professional football for eight different teams; three different leagues in two different countries (USA and Canada). His wife Laurie said, "When you are 6'-4" you have to prove you cannot play football but when you are 5'-10" you have to prove that you can play. Doug kept that mindset throughout his career."

You must commit to doing what it will take to succeed. Nobody else can decide for you.

So what's it going to be for you?

Take-Aways: Determination

Definition: firmly resolved; set in purpose or opinion; firmness of purpose.

Fruit: tenacity, intensity, passionate zeal, enthusiasm, perseverance, can-do spirit, teachability, focus, and a repentive heart

1. You must make up your mind up to stay the course before conflicts arise. "You have not yet resisted to the point of shedding blood in your striving against sin" (Heb. 12:4).

2. Possibility for greatness begins when your will is surrendered to Jesus (Gal. 2:20, Rom. 6).

3. The purity of your direction determines the strength of your resolve. (Is. 30:15)

4. The grateful three-dimensional athlete is the most resilient, impactful, and powerful athlete (Romans 12:1–2).

5. Determination requires mental toughness (Heb. 10:38–39).

6. Determination begins with commitment (1 Peter 4:1–2).

7. You cannot correct what you do not confront. Face your fears and face your pain as the first steps to maturity.

8. Determination can create enthusiasm that infects others.

Additional Scriptures: 1 Cor. 9:24, 16:1–14; 1 Peter 1:13–16, 5:5–10; Heb. 12: 1–12; Romans 5:3–5.

If you daily choose to Diligently practice your Disciplines with Determination in God's divine Direction and power (Diesel) using Discernment, then you will have a great Destiny.

Let's talk about Determination:

1. What do you rely on to motivate you day in and day out? (Col. 3:17, 23, Rom. 12:1–2)

2. What will it take for you to remain determined to accomplish your goals? (Read 1 Peter 1:13–16.)

3. What are some hurdles that you have experienced that you must overcome? (Read Heb. 12:1–3.)

4. How do you deal with setbacks, a bad performance, or disappointments? (Ps. 62, Lam. 3:22–26)

Chapter 3

DILIGENCE

"All right, men! Let's run it again!"
—any coach anywhere at any level at any time during practice

"But the precious possession of a man is diligence" (Prov. 12:27)NASB.

Rudy Ruettiger could have given up.

He was a forlorn, walk-on football player at Notre Dame who practiced all week but never played on Saturday—until the last game of his career.

With time running out, Ruettiger raced on the field at defensive end against Georgia Tech. On the final snap he bull-rushed, sacked the Yellow Jackets' quarterback, and rode away on the shoulders of euphoric teammates and the sound of Irish fans chanting, "Ru-dy! Ru-dy!"

It was believed to be only the second time in the storied history of Notre Dame football that a player had been carried off the field triumphantly.

It also was a life-changing tackle that sparked the popular movie, *Rudy,* and opened avenues to his career as a motivational speaker. Reflecting on the memorable sack years later, Ruettiger said that golden moment near the Golden Dome never would have happened if he had not practiced with great diligence every day.

—A.J. Carr

—PAT TEAGUE

Rudy was prepared for his moment because he diligently went to every practice with the heart to win and a proven work ethic.

I was a freshman in college when God revealed the truth of diligence to me. I was overwhelmed by the upper classmen's size, talent, and athletic maturity. My teammates were athletes like Perry Williams, who was an All-American defensive back and All-American sprinter at N.C. State. His work ethic was an example to all of us. He went on to be drafted by the New York Giants and played 11 years in the NFL. He holds the Giants' record for most consecutive starts at a defensive back position and earned two Super Bowl rings. Perry later earned his Master's in Public Administration from Fairleigh Dickinson University while playing professional football.

For me to ever play a down at NCSU, I needed some divine inspiration! So I cried out to God for wisdom on how to deal with my situation. I realized there was no way around one thing—hard work. I had to face the pain. This passage of Scripture opened my eyes to the value of hard work: "A lazy man does not roast his prey, **but the precious possession of a man is diligence**" (Prov. 12:27 NASB). I discovered a treasure! This diligence must become a precious possession in my daily routine.

Diligence is hard, consistent work. I had to get to work on the disciplines that had been presented to me. There was no magic vitamin that could get me there. I had to trust God with what was out of my control and get busy doing what I knew I must do. I learned a valuable lesson. We all need to remember -- **There is no shortcut to the top, only preparation and perspiration!**

If we are slack in preparation, we will not recognize our opportunity. If we are lazy, the competition will pass us by. We will not "roast our prey" if we are waiting for our opposition to come to us, as by that time we have already lost our moment of opportunity. The wise one works hard while the lazy one sleeps away his hour of opportunity (Prov. 10:5). Diligence is essential if we are to be ready to respond to the moment when our team needs us to help win the game.

I learned this first-hand during my redshirt senior year at NC State. The summer before my fourth year, I was not diligent in off-season workouts. I had worked hard during all the previous summers and reaped great benefits from it. If I had continued on the pace I had set, I could have broken the record for most tackles in the school's history. However, I lost sight of my goals that summer and spent more time with my girlfriend than with my teammates in the weight room and on the track. For some reason, I thought that just going through the motions of working out would get me the same results as before. I was plagued with nagging injuries all season due to a lack of summer preparation. My contribution to the team was half the production from the previous year. The principle of diligence or hard work applies to everyone -- no one is exempt! It's like the law of gravity—it doesn't matter who we are;

if we walk off a ten-story building, we will either be dead or seriously hurt when we land. We will not float down on our good intentions.

Please do not make the same mistake I made. Diligence requires intensity, persistence, and a conscientious, consistent, intentional effort. Willie Mays (Hall of Fame Baseball player) said it is easy to be good for a day, but you've got to be good every day.

When we carry out the discipline required for our position, we will see the results. Just as "the eye in the sky" (the camera) doesn't lie, so goes our performance, which directly affects our contribution to the team and the coaches' confidence in putting us in the game. We must not blame our coach for not starting us when we know in our hearts we did not put forth the effort on the practice field to turn potential into production.

When a coach sees a player diligently practicing their disciplines, the coach realizes that he can depend on that player when the pressure is on to make a big play for the team. You may not be the most talented player, but you can be the most consistent or the most reliable through diligence.

If we make diligence an important play in our life, then we will press on when we are tempted to give in to fatigue or discouragement. The good habits formed through consistent practice will instinctively kick in to pull you through. Tim Tebow showed us how it's done in the 2011 football season with the Denver Broncos when he led them through seven come-from-behind victories. He said, "Hard work beats talent when talent doesn't work hard."

When hard times or adversity hits, we can become even more enthusiastic and diligent because we "know that tribulation brings about perseverance and perseverance creates proven character and proven character births hope (not hype—my words here) and hope does not disappoint because the love of God has been poured out within our hearts through the Holy Spirit who was given to us" (Rom. 5:3–5).

With diligence, we see a progression of development that begins with persevering, testing, and practicing. Perseverance requires pressing on even when it hurts. Perseverance produces something most needed in every part of life—character.

Character comes only from repetition of proper action when one is confronted by adversity or opposition. For example, when you are confronted with adversity, do you face up to it or do you run away from it? Are you *a* character or do you *have* character? There is a big difference when others are depending on you. If you have character, you know you're prepared when it is time to perform. When you consistently display character, then only results that give birth to hope will occur. You will experience God's great love from the inside out. "In all labor there is profit, but mere talk leads to poverty" (Prov. 14:23).

This principle of diligence is where direction, determination, and discipline all come together to be practiced so you can be prepared to succeed during the game or in life. Your game-time habits are a reflection of our practice-time habits.

When you integrate the winning play of diligence into your athletic regimen, it carries over into other areas of your life. Diligent and consistent study or work habits lead to success in school or in the workplace. In the words of Samuel Johnson, "What we hope ever to do with ease we must first learn to do with diligence."

Being a good "farmer" is our first occupation when it comes to diligence. If we are sowing seeds of consistent, intentional work on our disciplines, we will reap a harvest of excellence. If we sow seeds of mindless routine, we will reap a harvest of mediocrity and lost opportunities.

I was once asked to speak to 150 hockey-crazed eight-, nine-, and ten-year-old boys. I asked them, "If a farmer plants corn in the field, what will he get?"

A bunch of hands went up quickly, and I called on one, who answered, "Fiber?"

After a good laugh, I told the group you would reap corn if you sowed corn seeds! Therefore, if you sow seeds of diligent hard work, you will reap a harvest of excellence, confidence, and success. Keep it simple and get busy planting! Stop analyzing, it is paralyzing.

Once we have our disciplines, we must practice them diligently until we become experts at what we do. If we practice those disciplines diligently, then destiny is just around the corner.

Take-Aways: Diligence

Definition: The practice of doing something over and over again until you get it right and then continuing to do it (incisive, sharp, clear, intentional); conscientiously and consistently practicing a discipline (accumulated knowledge in a certain area).

Fruit: Excellence, consistency, resilience, prosperity, faithfulness, patience, willingness to receive instruction.

1. You reap what you sow, so you must be a good farmer. Plant seeds of hard work, and you will reap a harvest of excellence and success (Gal. 6:7–9).

2. Diligence will put us in place of leadership (Prov. 12:24).

3. Diligence will help us overcome temptation (Prov. 4:23).

4. Diligence is the key to improving our disciplines (2 Peter 1:3–10).

5. Diligence is translated into hard work (Prov. 10:4, 13:4).

6. There's no shortcut to the top; there is only preparation and perspiration (Prov. 21:5).

Additional Scriptures: Prov. 13:4, 8:17, 10:4, 21:5

If you daily choose to Diligently practice your Disciplines with Determination in God's divine Direction and power (Diesel) using Discernment, then you will have a great Destiny.

Let's Talk about Diligence:

1. What does diligence mean to you?

2. Is there a discipline you have been practicing diligently? What has been the result?

3. What practical habit do you need to implement into your training regimen?

4. What are you afraid of when it comes to hard work?

5. What spiritual disciplines do you need to practice diligently in order to have a more intimate relationship with Jesus?

6. How do you see diligence benefitting you?

7. Which disciplines do you need to practice diligently to make you a better person?

Chapter 4

DISCIPLINE

"The difference between the good and great
players is that the great ones love to do what the good ones hate to do."
—Coach John Wooden

"Hit it" with Discipline

Boys and men can learn much from their mothers, sisters, girlfriends, and wives. World-renowned water-skier Kristi Overton-Johnson has demonstrated the importance of faith and discipline in her sport. —PT

There were days when Kristi Overton-Johnson did not want to get wet, didn't feel like strapping on skis, jumping ramps, and practicing water tricks.

She did all that anyway.

Day after day she grabbed the towrope, hollered "Hit it!" to her driver, and swerved and splashed across the lake.

The consistent effort paid off. After countless drills, spills, and thrills, Overton-Johnson set national records, turned pro at age thirteen, and eventually became the premier female water-skier in the world.

"I loved the sport, had a desire to achieve, to be the best I could be," said Overton-Johnson, who began skiing at age four.

Plenty of days her body hurt, and she would have preferred cooling it instead of hitting it. Yet every day she made the decision to holler "Hit it!" and keep sharpening her skiing skills on the shimmering lake.

That determination, diligence, and discipline, blended with God-given talent, propelled Overton-Johnson to a career that left numerous records rippling in her wake. Her resume includes 80 pro slalom victories, eight US Masters titles, four US Open championships, multiple number-one world rankings and pain as well as fame. She underwent ten surgeries.

More importantly, Overton-Johnson has used her athletic fame to acclaim Christ to thousands through *In His Wakes*, a Christian ministry she founded in 2003 and has been actively involved with husband, Tim Johnson. An attorney and mother of three children, Overton-Johnson also has written several Bible studies and shares her faith as a widely sought Christian speaker.

"My calling is to 'Hit it!' with God," said Overton-Johnson, whose true power source isn't a ski boat or towrope, but her heavenly Father.

—A.J. Carr

"Whoever loves discipline loves knowledge …" (Prov. 12:1).

—PAT TEAGUE

What field of knowledge do we need to study to master our positions? The only way to begin this journey is to define and refine the disciplines we need in order to be successful. The disciplines can be spiritual, athletic, academic, or professional. Our ability to execute a discipline is the most critical of the seven plays.

Discipline is the practice of accumulated knowledge in our field of expertise at the right time, at the right place, and with excellence. Discipline is what we must practice diligently with great determination and direction.

For example, if I am a linebacker, I must perfect the art of making tackles, shedding a blocker, reading offensive formations, analyzing film on the opponent, recognizing down and distance tendencies, calling a blitz or a stunt, and quickly reading whether it's a run, draw or a pass play, to name just a few disciplines.

As we gather knowledge and begin to execute appropriately, we will succeed. Do not misunderstand this principle or you can imprison yourself, as disciplines are designed to liberate us to success, not to confine us to a meaningless regimen. For example, the huddle is not why we play football or why we watch the game. (No one ever said, "Wow, let's go watch my team huddle for four quarters.") The huddle is the discipline of communicating the play in order to win the game. Another example is nutrition. There is an enormous amount of knowledge to accumulate on nutrition to optimize your health. You could be so wrapped up in the regiment of counting calories that you lose focus on why you are doing it. It's not about what you can't eat, it's about choosing the right fuel to free your body to perform better. This discipline can liberate you to get in the best shape of your life. How could discipline confine me? When you lose focus, on the "why" you are practicing a discipline and you torment yourself when you miss it. When you center your whole world on a discipline rather than the purpose of the discipline, then you fall into condemnation. How can I turn that into liberation? Liberation comes when your decisions are no longer based on your emotions, appetites or your ego. Your decisions are based on irrefutable absolute timeless truths rather than on how you feel at the moment. There are winning disciplines for life such as listening, self-control, service to name a few. There is much to say on this topic for another day or another book! Therefore, the disciplines are the tools used to execute the plan or purpose to achieve your destiny.

The Secret of How to Go from Good to Great

Discipline is not easy (Heb. 12:11). It goes against your natural desire to take the path of least resistance and avoid conflict or pain. As a parent, I have to tell my children to do some things they do not want to do but for their benefit.

As a teenager, two teammates and I were invited to a 5-Star basketball camp in the Pocono Mountains in western Pennsylvania, led by legendary UCLA coach John Wooden, winner of ten NCAA Men's Division I National Championships. I was in awe of all the great coaches and players who were there with Coach Wooden. I remember whenever Coach Wooden walked into the gym, a hush came over the crowd for a moment before another level of intensity erupted like a rock band exploding with their opening number onstage. The coaches coached louder, and the players played harder. The energy generated in those moments could light a city!

Every time Coach Wooden held a workshop session, players and coaches alike took notes. I remember Coach saying, "I have been around a lot of good players and great players, but I found what makes the difference is that the great players love to do what good players hate to do." It was the greatest nugget of truth, and if I had not been listening, I would have missed the secret of going from good to great. Coach Wooden then asked us to make a list of things we hated to do and challenged us to learn to love them if we wanted to be great. Along with all the other players, I quickly wrote down my list: homework, jump rope, wind sprints, squats, and suicides.

In other words, you choose your pain and your pleasures. If you face the pain and combat laziness, you will enjoy the pleasure of eventually achieving your goal. Another great athlete, who is in agreement with Coach Wooden, is NFL Hall of Fame wide receiver Jerry Rice, who said, "Today I will do what others won't, so tomorrow I can accomplish what others can't." This secret transformed my athletic career. The following season my teammates and I experienced the first undefeated season in our school's basketball history.

Remember, discipline is knowledge in a specific area exercised with expertise and timing. Your discipline could take you around the world 27 times and into 85 countries. That is exactly what happened in the life of Ralph C. Meloon, Sr. who turned 99 years old in 2016! He has traveled the world promoting Correct Craft and Nautique boats and teaching water skiing. He and his family founded Correct Craft in 1925. Ralph was the first ski boat driver for the famous Cypress Garden Water Ski shows. Through his leadership, the first water ski team was formed in the United States.

Once we have our disciplines, we must practice them diligently until we achieve excellence -- then our destiny is just around the corner! The ultimate destiny is to hear from our heavenly Father, "Well done, good and faithful servant. You have fought the good fight of faith." Everyone wants to hear that from his or her heavenly Father and feel that joy from the Spirit.

Take-Aways: Discipline

Definition: Doing the right thing when you don't feel like it. Practicing accumulated knowledge with excellence and the right timing.

Fruit: Excellence, achievement, satisfaction, peaceful fruit of righteousness, willingness to accept instruction, constructive action (i.e. training, drills) correct execution of knowledge

1. Discipline is choosing your pain and your pleasure (Luke 9:23).

2. Short-term pain = long-term pleasure. Short-term pleasure = long-term pain. This is your daily choice (1 Cor. 15:33).

   "All discipline for the moment seems not to be joyful, but sorrowful; yet to those who have been trained by it, afterwards it yields the peaceful fruit of righteousness" (Heb. 12:11).

3. Train your body to become an instrument or vessel to carry out your commands. Coach John Wooden said, "Great players love to do what good players hate to do," So list what you hate to do and learn to love them.

4. Everyone needs discipline (Heb. 5:8). "Although [Jesus] was a Son, He learned obedience through the things He suffered" (Heb. 12:1–13).

5. Some disciplines can be defined by your parents, teachers, directors, pastors, and coaches (Prov. 12:1, 23:12). "Apply your heart to discipline [instruction], and your ears to words of knowledge" (Prov. 19:27).

6. Disciplines are designed to liberate you to success, not to confine you to a meaningless regimen. (1 Cor. 9:24–27).

If you daily choose to Diligently practice your Disciplines with Determination in God's divine Direction and power (Diesel) using Discernment, then you will have a great Destiny.

Let's Talk about Discipline:

1. What disciplines do you need to practice in order to be successful?

2. Recall a challenging time in your life. What did you learn during that time?

3. What is on your list of things that you hate to do that you know will make you better at what you do?

4. What are the basics disciplines of the role you play? How about your position?

5. How do the disciplines you practice in your role relate to other areas of your life? In school? At work? In relationships?

6. What spiritual disciplines do you need to practice in order to have a more intimate relationship with Jesus?

Chapter 5

DISCERNMENT

"You are here." —any GPS

In the world of college football, legendary coach Bear Bryant was known for his hound's-tooth hat and winning—most notably winning.

However, in the early 1970s, his Alabama teams experienced uncommon slippage with consecutive 6-win seasons, a poor record in Bear's book. That's when he considered changing to the Wishbone offense popularized by Darrell Royal's successful Texas squads.

Tide assistant coaches were assigned to study the Longhorns' scheme, which they did, and Alabama installed that offense the following season.

The offensive switch helped put Alabama back in elite status and the Tide rolled past opponents who wished they didn't have to see the Wishbone. Talented athletes on both sides of the ball and stellar overall play also factored into the resurgence, but changing the offense was one of the significant moves in the team's turnaround.

Had Bryant lacked discernment or been too obstinate to change, the Tide might have languished in mediocrity again. Bryant wasn't about mediocrity. He had won at Maryland, Kentucky, and Texas A&M before creating a national power in Tuscaloosa. His four teams combined amassed a then record 323 victories, including six national championships and 13 conference titles at Alabama.

As a young reporter, I was somewhat intimidated when waiting to interview Bryant by phone before his Alabama team played Duke many years ago. This was "The Bear." Would he answer every question with a growl?

No, he spoke with a soft, Southern drawl and kindly made complimentary remarks about Duke.

A few days later, his Crimson Tide wasn't so kind to the Blue Devils, rambling to victory in decisive, Bear-like fashion.

—A.J. Carr

"...who because of practice have their senses trained to discern good and evil" (Heb. 5:14)

—PAT TEAGUE

Using discernment will help us evaluate where we are in the journey and what it's going to take to get us to our destination.

Discernment is our GPS on our journey to destiny. Ask yourself this question: *Can I be honest with myself about where I am? **We can deceive ourselves into thinking we are on course because we have the tendency to judge ourselves by our intentions rather by what we have actually accomplished.*** Deception can come in the form of self-centered, rather than team-centered, thinking. You can choose to *allow* yourself to be deceived because you do not want to be inconvenienced with the truth (which leads to blaming your shortcomings on anyone but yourself). When we are willing to make a scapegoat out of someone else, regardless of the harm we cause to that person, that is evil.

Remember the story about Vernon Davis in Chapter 1? Transform your mind so that it does not yield to an unsatisfying, lustful appetite for personal glory or listen to limitations created by your critics. Critics' opinions can force you into a box made of walls of excuses. Coach Singletary delivered his instruction in such a way that Vernon was able to receive it and change.

As a Coach, you should choose wisely how you deliver your message from a standpoint that you know an athlete is better than what they are settling for. Condemnation can tear down the athlete through condescending accusations and statements of limitations. Frustration can cause a coach to resort to this kind of coaching. On the other hand, you can intensely challenge them through your belief they are better than what you just witnessed on the field.

As a player, regardless of how you receive instruction, choose to have a teachable spirit. There is a vast difference between receiving instruction with a mindset of determination to improve and choosing to receive instruction negatively as criticism. Instruction convinces you to improve, to break down those walls of excuses, and eventually to accomplish the goal. In the real world, you can't choose how you're going to get the instruction you need to improve. In other words, find the meat in the instruction and spit out the bones. Discernment can help you determine the difference so you can recognize where you are falling short and where you are making progress. Your relentless desire to be the best you can be should drive away a whiney attitude regarding the way the instruction was delivered. Grow up, forgive, and move on!

In 2013, the San Antonio Spurs were narrowly beaten by the invincible Miami Heat with Lebron James, Dwayne Wade, and Chris Bosh in the NBA championship series. Some critics said the Spurs were finished as a championship team because the players and coach were too old. However, the resilient Spurs coach, Greg Popovich, and his players and team leaders (Tim Duncan, Tony Parker, and Manu Ginobili) didn't let that criticism destroy their resolve.

They used discernment to improve their overall teamwork. They asked the hard questions. What was the result? They got a rematch in 2014 with the same powerful Miami Heat team still featuring superhuman, Lebron James, only this time the Spurs beat the Heat and won the title.

Why did I lose the starting position? Did I run ten forty-yard sprints in my designated times or not? If not, why did I miss my times? Was it because I was out of shape? I must be willing to ask the hard questions and not cast blame on someone else. I must confront the real issues, knowing I cannot correct what I do not confront. Admit, confess, and decide on a new plan of action and execute the plan.

Stop right here and exercise this principle.

What did I find out? Did I write it down? Admitting where I fall short is the first step to positive change. Did I make a decision to exercise a new plan to combat my weakness? Did I write that down?

If our determination is low, then our direction may need clarifying, and if our disciplines are not sharp, then our diligent practice habits may have become inconsistent.

Let's apply this to our spiritual life. Second Corinthians 13:5 states, "Examine ourselves to see whether we are in the faith; test ourselves." If we are not at peace with God, then what stands in our way? Confess the sin that easily entangles our feet so we can run the race in such a way that we may win (Heb. 12:1–3).

Why hinder ourselves from winning? We must deal with our own mess (1 John 1:9, Hebrews 12:1–2, 1 Corinthians 9:24).

We need wise counsel to assist us in the discerning process. Getting such counsel begins with developing a prayer life with the ultimate coach to guide us. Discernment begins when we begin to seek the truth. Remember that the truth will set us free to get on with living (John 8:32). Our hearts are fickle, which leaves them open to deception (Jer. 17:9), so we must rely on the one who created us and the owner's manual, the Bible, to reveal where we are on our journey. My sister Bonnie once told me, "Let the Bible read you instead of you reading the Bible."

You may have seen a mall directory that lists all the stores' locations. The "you are here" sticker lets you know where you are in relation to where you want to go. Discernment is the "you are here" sticker in the directory of life. Look at yourself honestly and see where you are today in relation to where you want to be a year from now, five years from now, and ten years from now. Taking the time to self-reflect in this way and run the play of discernment is critical in being able to determine where you are on life's journey in fulfilling your destiny.

Another aspect of discernment is training your senses to discern what is good and what is evil. Evil can come in the form of self-centered thinking, rather than God-centered thinking. Let your mind be transformed, rather than conformed to your critics (Romans 12:1–2). Rejoice in the fact that God is at work in you, as this will ignite your heart to press on to the God's call for excellence (Philippians 3:12–14).

Let us train our senses by meditating on God's Word (Psalm 1). Watch the "game film" of your life by being alone with God so He can show you things through the trainer, the Holy Spirit (John 14:26, 15:26, 16:13).

God can also lead us to talk with a reliable, godly friend who can assist us in discerning what are the right things to do to continue to grow and improve, and the greatest friend and helper is the Holy Spirit. Jesus told us that the Holy Spirit will be a Teacher, a Helper, a Reminder, and a Comforter. The Holy Spirit is the part of the Godhead that leads you to realize you need a Savior. He will also help you discern what is good and bad, right and wrong, righteous and evil.

When I exercise with weights, I like to have a good, attentive spotter when I am going to "lift heavy". In the same way, I see the Holy Spirit constantly walking along side me to spot me when the weight of stress becomes heavy. "But the Helper, the Holy Spirit, whom the Father will send in My name, He will teach you all things, and bring to your remembrance all that I said to you" (John 14:26). Once I access His help, He will guide me to the kind of people who will encourage me on my journey.

Take-Aways: Discernment

Definition: The quality of being able to comprehend what is obscure; the skill of discerning; keen perception into human motives; discrimination; the power to distinguish and select what is true, appropriate, or excellent; good judgment pertaining to subject matter overlooked by others; wisdom

Fruit: insight, motivation, conviction, encouragement, sober spirit, liberty, peace, revelation

1. Discernment is born when we are serious about seeking and pursuing truth (John 8:32). " … and you know the truth and the truth will set you free" (Prov. 2:1–22).

2. Train your senses by meditating on God's Word (Ps. 1).

3. You must know where you are before you can get where you are going (Prov. 14:12, 16:25; 1 Corinthians 12:9).

4. Discernment comes from God (Josh. 1:1–10).

5. Our senses should be trained to discern what is good and what is evil by using universal, absolute truths (Heb. 5:14–6:1–3).

6. God-centered thinking gives us perspective on life, relationships, and circumstances (2 Corinthians 4:16–18).

7. You must discern where you are before you can get to where you need to be.

8. Discern between what is instructional coaching for unlimited success and what are critical accusations that create limitations.

If you daily choose to Diligently practice your Disciplines with Determination in God's divine Direction and power (Diesel) using Discernment, then you will have a great Destiny.

Let's Talk about Discernment:

1. Have you allowed Jesus to give you direction in your life as the head coach of your life, or is He just an advisor?

2. Can you determine where you are on this journey? Read Prov. 14:12 and 16:25. What do these verses mean to you?

3. Read Jeremiah 29:11 and Proverbs 3:5–6. How do you get God's direction for your life?

4. What are your goals in life--spiritually, mentally, and physically?

5. Which area—direction, determination, diligence, or discipline—is your strongest? Which is your weakest?

6. What role do you think wise counsel could play in your discernment?

7. Give examples of where discernment made a difference in your life or where you observed it making an impact in others' lives. Give an example of where a lack of discernment affected you or others.

8. What do you want out of life?

Chapter 6

DESTINY

"The Bear Hug"

Jeremiah 29:11 "'For I know the plans that I have for you,' declares the LORD ..."

(Jer. 29:11).

Lennie Rosenbluth was a skinny kid seemingly chasing the Impossible Dream. Growing up in New York, he struggled to make a school basketball team and was cut from his seventh-, eighth, ninth, and tenth-grade squads.

Undaunted, Rosenbluth persevered, playing in church and YMCA leagues, plus at a high-profile summer camp, where he caught the attention of a few college coaches. That led to a tryout at NC State, but he failed to impress legendary Wolfpack coach Everett Case.

"I didn't have any shoes," Rosenbluth remembers. "He gave me shoes (but) I got blisters, wasn't in shape, couldn't run. He said Coach Case told him: 'I can't use you. I can't waste a scholarship on you.'

"I don't blame him," Rosenbluth said. "I didn't show him anything."

Well, not that day.

Frank McGuire, who was leaving St. John's for the head-coaching position at North Carolina, knew about Rosenbluth's talent and offered the New Yorker a scholarship. Good investment!

Rosenbluth rose to All-America status and won National Player of the Year honors in 1957, when he led the Tar Heels to a perfect 32–0 season and the NCAA championship that culminated with a triple-overtime upset win over Wilt Chamberlain's Kansas Jayhawks.

One of the sharpest shooters in college basketball, Rosenbluth vexed opponents with a lightning-quick jumper and a sometimes sweeping hook. With those skills and a "never give up" mindset (Determination; winning play #2), he averaged 28 points per game in 1957, a single-season Tar Heel record that was still standing as of 2017.

—A.J. Carr

—PAT TEAGUE

The ultimate destiny is "The Bear Hug."

This happens when life has been lived to the fullest, and we are called to heaven. In my mind's eye, we are ushered into the stadium of heaven and it is full. Jesus sees us, gives each one of us "the bear hug," and I imagine Him saying something like, "Well done, my good and faithful servant. You have fought the good fight of faith." I picture Him lifting our hands up, and the stadium lets out a thunderous cheer. Our hearts are flooded with joy and gratitude!

Psalm 139:14 states that you were "fearfully and wonderfully made", and Psalm 139:18 states that His thoughts about you outnumber the sand on the beach. You are not a mistake; you have a calling and a purpose, there is a reason that He made you! No one else is like you. No one has your fingerprints. You are a top recruit at your position, and Jesus has recruited you to play on His team. You have been chosen, but it's up to you to accept the invitation. We need each person to play his/her position, as no one else can play it. Each person is one play away from fulfilling his or her destiny.

A kind word at the right time and in the right spirit can change a life. This is why we train our spirits to take the lead. Our minds/souls and bodies execute "the play," and the Spirit of God does something supernatural in someone's life. This originates from a belief that every person is valuable and a priceless treasure waiting to be realized. Peyton Manning said this in his announcement of his retirement, "Treat a man as he is and he will remain as he is. Treat a man as he could be and he will become the man he should be."

Destiny is just one play away. For example, the NY Giants would not have made it to the 2012 Super Bowl if it were not for #15 doing his job on the punt team. His two fumble recoveries on two different punts resulted in a ten-point swing in the game. He is now a part of NFL lore. He achieved his destiny as a player. His name is Devon Thomas.

We are also one play away from our destiny. If we choose to practice our spiritual disciplines diligently today, we may see an opportunity to share with someone how they, too, can have a relationship with Jesus the Christ. The opportunity may also be as simple as being kind to someone, which could be a game-changer in that person's life. Devon Thomas may not have thought that being a "cover guy" on the punt team could make much of an impact on the game, but it did! What if he had decided to slack off that play because he was tired of being double-teamed?

Destiny is when it all comes together. It is like a baseball player hitting a home run in the bottom of the 9th inning, or a running back breaking free to score the winning touchdown, a basketball player making the winning shot at the buzzer, a goalie making the save to preserve a win, or a surfer who catches the ultimate wave!

Let's put in perspective; in life no one can play the position God has designed only you to play. He has put a great deal of time and thought into how He made each of us.

Our fingerprints are unique; in fact, only fourteen points must line up for the FBI to match it. Don't believe anyone who has said you are a mistake or that you are some random piece of evolutionary matter. Each one of us has been specially made by God for a specific purpose and with a specific destiny to impact our generation. As part of this generation, I need each one of you on my team. I cannot play your position. No one else can because you have been divinely designed to play it. It's never too late to step up. In the Bible, King David fulfilled his purpose for his generation in spite of terrible mistakes (Acts 13:36). We can too!

Destiny can also refer to accomplishing your goals. We learn so much on this journey. The sacrifices we make to get where we are going can be offerings back to God for giving us the talents and skills to get it done (Col. 3:17).

Many athletes have accomplished much more than I have, but the lessons I learned from my journey and the relationships I developed are priceless. My high school teammates and I still get together because the bonds we forged on the field turned into lasting friendship off the field through Christ. The following are a few great examples of some my close high school friends and teammates applying these winning plays today on the field of life to fulfill their destiny. First, Dr. Lance Plyler, the Medical Director of the Disaster Response Unit at Samaritan's Purse, was God's instrument to save the lives of Dr. Kent Brantly and Nurse Nancy Writebol when they tested positive for the Ebola virus while ministering to thousands in Liberia (Chronicled in the movie called "Piercing the Darkness"). Next, Darrell Roberts is the Senior Pastor of Harvest House Church in Boone, North Carolina where he has faithfully served for over 30 years and ministered in 19 different countries. Another example is in the life of John Adams who is a successful executive/entrepreneur/philanthropist overcoming his ongoing battle with Parkinson's disease. He is an inspirational example of a true disciple of Jesus Christ mentoring his employees to go for a higher standard. Andy Shaffer is a Senior Pastor at The Journey Church in Dunn, North Carolina making a lasting impact in that community. There are many other teammates from High School like successful businessman, Kevin DeVries, and Pediatric Cardiologist, Dr. Jon Donnelly, my workout-training buddies growing up who made an impact on my life and many others. My high school teammates and I began to see our destinies unfold when we decided to follow Jesus's example and not the norms of popular culture. We experienced a move of God that changed the culture of our school. My friends and I used the platform of athletics to reach our peers through the Fellowship of Christian Athletes (FCA). We had a blast doing it—highs with no hangovers!

My college teammates (some of whom are mentioned earlier in this book) and I enjoy annual reunions to continue our journey. One of my prayer partners from college, Mack McKeithan, is one the most resilient people I know. He was a great baseball player and athlete. Mack is the embodiment of the joy of the Lord. He would come by my dorm room after a rough day of practice and lift my spirit up out of the dumps. He is now the President of ProMATIC Automation Inc., a supplier of custom industrial automation services and equipment worldwide. My senior year at NC State, Scott Auer (my roommate), Mack and I were leaders together at Fellowship of Christian Athletes (FCA) where we developed lifelong friendship/brotherhood and enjoyed seeing God change many lives. Also, I developed lasting friendships through my professional football experience as well. Cazzy Francis, a Wide Receiver from Arkansas State University, was my roommate at the Tampa Bay Buccaneers. He is also a great example of someone who is running the winning plays for life. He is now the Senior Pastor at Pathway Church Mid County in Nederland, Texas being a "receiver" of God's Word.

Enjoy where you are today, and quit worrying about tomorrow. Seize this moment today that God has given you to fulfill your destiny now.

Take-Aways: Destiny

Definition: Fate; the predetermined course of events; a destination

Fruit: Fulfillment, satisfaction, a sense of accomplishment, gratitude toward the heavenly Father

1. Destiny is part of your reward in life (James 1:12).

2. Destiny is when you are in the "sweet spot" of what you were born to do (Ps. 139).

3. Destiny is fulfilling your purpose in your generation (Acts 13:36).

4. The ultimate destiny is "the bear hug" (Matt. 25:21–23, Luke 19:17, 2 Tim. 4:7, 1 Tim. 1:18, 6:12).

5. You are always one "play" away from fulfilling your destiny (1 Peter 1:13).

6. God has planned a great future for your life that gives you hope now and forever (Jer. 29:11–13, Prov. 3:5–6).

7. The winning plays for life get you in position to make that game-changing play.

If you daily choose to Diligently practice your Disciplines with Determination in God's divine Direction and power (Diesel) using Discernment, then you will have a great Destiny.

Let's Talk about Destiny:

1. Have you allowed Jesus to give you direction as the head coach of your life, or is He just an advisor?

2. What have you learned so far about your destiny?

3. Read Jer. 29:11–13. What is the main thing you need to do to be in position to achieve your destiny?

4. Have you accomplished any of your goals in life? What are your goals? List five long-term and five short-term goals.

5. What are you doing to influence your generation?

Chapter 7

THE DIESEL! –
GRACE - POWER

***GRACERADE**: Is it in you?*

There are days on the PGA tour when a golfer's drives soar long and straight and birdie putts keep falling. There also are days when shots go awry, when the ball lands in bunkers and water hazards and the putts stop short or roll long, creating grief on the greens.

Webb Simpson, a former Wake Forest All-America who joined the tour in 2008, knows all about the fun — and the frustration. In his first 229 tournaments, Simpson missed the cut 60 times.

More impressively, he won 4 tour championships, including the 2012 U.S.Open, and posted 49 Top 10 finishes. In this fickle game, Simpson is steadied and strengthened by his Christian faith, which he shares unabashedly. It is what helps him stay humble in victory and determined amid the storms of adversity.

During a CBS Sports interview after claiming his 2011 Wyndham title, Simpson thanked "my Lord and Savior Jesus Christ," and noted how he felt God's "presence" during the last, nerve-wracking 18 holes. Simpson, married and father of four children, speaks at various events such as Fellowship of Christian Athletes meetings, is involved with the College Golf Fellowship ministry, supports charities and gives God the glory.

—A.J. Carr

"For the grace of God has appeared, bringing salvation to all men" **(Titus 2:11)**

—PAT TEAGUE

I love the 2007 Gatorade commercial with Peyton Manning, Dwayne Wade, Maria Sharapova, and Derek Jeter, with Jerry Goldsmith's dramatic music in the background. The scoreboard flashes "00:27" and then the words, "When all seems lost and the whole world is watching, who will come through when it matters most?"

As time ticks off the scoreboard clock, several athletes are individually highlighted making a dramatic, game-changing play, hit, shot, or pass that wins the game. The music intensifies, the chorus soars, and the words flash on the screen, "Every game needs a hero. Is it in you?" Then the celebration of triumph begins. *I love it!*

So I'll ask you this question, *"Gracerade – Is it IN you?"* Is God's grace in you to energize your spirit, soul and body? You can confidently ask for

His grace at any time or any place. When your body needs a boost -- a Gatorade can rehydrate you. When your spirit needs a boost, the grace of God can "rehydrate" your spirit.

The Gatorade commercial also captures our desire to be the hero. Who doesn't want to be the one to come through with the big play for his or her team? How about coming through in life's everyday challenges and temptations? Are we going to step up? Let's explore what needs to be *in* you.

All of the principles we have discussed can create a game-changing vehicle by which you can impact the world. Comprehending the need to apply the "6Ds" to your life can be a life-changing revelation. As you begin to choose to practice your disciplines daily with diligence, determination, discernment, and focused direction, you will realize that these principles are a powerful, game-changing vehicle that will help you achieve your destiny. I realized I could go only so far in the vehicle that is my body pushing it by myself. I was burning out, losing steam and momentum. My vehicle needed some gas! The grace of God is the gas that got it moving.

You may even want to call this the seventh "D," diesel fuel. If you look back at our central statement, it has been there all along.

*If you daily choose to Diligently practice your Disciplines with Determination in God's divine Direction and **power (Diesel – the Grace of God)** using Discernment, then you will have a great Destiny.*

Without His grace, the diesel fuel, there is no sustainable, enabling power to continue the journey. Do not rely on your own ability, but in the God who has the power to save.

I realized that I was not winning my battles with sin, so I tried repeatedly to control my behavior using determination. Next, I tried applying certain disciplines that a friend or a book had recommended. I still did not consistently win against sin. Finally, while reading Romans 7, I had a revelation – I could not control my behavior using my natural instincts and my own efforts, but must instead rely upon Jesus' ability and His triumph over sin. "For by grace you have been saved through faith; and that not of yourselves, it is a gift of God not as a result of works, so that no one may boast" (Ephesians 2:8–9). It is about what Jesus has already done not about what I can do.

I can only access this gift through faith to receive the grace I need. "Therefore let us draw near with confidence to the throne of grace, so that we may receive mercy and find grace to help in time of need" (Heb. 4:16). Therefore, the discipline to practice diligently comes from relying on Jesus' victory over sin and His power (grace) to enable you to overcome. In other words, do not rely on your ability to behave in a certain way but on His proven ability to save. "Therefore let us be diligent to enter that rest, so that no one will fall, through *following* the same example of disobedience" (Heb. 4:11).

"Thanks be to God who leads us in HIS triumph ..." (1 Corinthians 2:14). We should be living from a place of victory not trying to get victory. My prayer for you and me is that we discover this powerful truth so we do not lose heart, grow weary in doing good, and quit before we achieve our destinies.

There should not be a place in our vocabulary for the word "quit." We have an adversary whose goals are to kill us, steal our dreams, and destroy our destinies, so remember to rely on the superior source for your motivation and strength to go on. James 4:7-8 in the Bible says, "Submit therefore to God. Resist the devil and he will flee from you. Draw near to God and He will draw near to you." When I read this, I get a picture of some type of temptation knocking on the door of my heart, but I resist the devil by submitting to God – making Him the master of my heart. I draw near to God by acknowledging Him in my every day activities. So I am living with God and not just living for God. I believe that is the big difference between being religious and being in a relationship with God. For example, when discouragement knocks on the door of my heart, I imagine myself walking away from that door and allowing Jesus to answer it instead (because He's the Head Coach of my heart). I draw near to God by occupying my thoughts with scripture, a song, or a constructive task that will glorify God. Jesus, the Word made flesh, is greater than any discouragement that comes knocking—there is no contest. He defeats discouragement and replaces it with faith and hope.

However, in this same illustration, if I try to open the door to discouragement and battle in my own power and with my own words, I will be knocked on my back looking through the earhole of my helmet wondering what happened. God equips us with the Sword of the Spirit—His promises in His Word to aggressively combat the enemy of our soul at the right time. The grace of God will empower us to focus on the discipline at hand and to practice diligently in order to accomplish what needs to be done.

I know this because that is what has happened to me too many times. You must allow Jesus to deal with discouragement through His victories. You and I need to resist the initial temptation to battle on the front where God has already won and instead submit to God, who supplies all the grace (James 4:7–8). Our battle is to take the deceitful lies of the enemy entering our minds captive by using the knowledge of who God is (All-Powerful) and replacing my convoluted plan of action with Jesus' plan of action (WWJD – What would Jesus Do) if He were confronted with my situation. (2 Corinthians 10:3-5). Believing who I am through Jesus Christ gives me the confidence to exercise my authority over the spiritual forces of darkness.

Then draw near to God in a faith-filled prayer of thanksgiving because He has given us everything pertaining to life and godliness (1 Peter 1:3–4). Then you can continue on your way, having escaped a moment of temptation.

If you or I rely on another source to help cope with our struggles, that source will sooner or later fail, and there will likely be a terrible side effect. If you use drugs, alcohol, or the like, it will destroy your engine. Without grace, our spirit will be depleted and we will begin to cramp up like athletes who have not stayed hydrated in an intense game. So ask for the *"Gracerade"* of God!

There's a way that seems right to a man but its end is the way of death" (Prov. 16:25). No other source will last as long as His grace. You and I need to make up our minds to trust in it fully because anything less will eventually become depleted. Grace is the premium fuel that will make our engines run most efficiently. We can confidently ask for this grace at any time or place (Heb. 4:16). There is an endless supply. When we begin to understand all God has done for us through Christ, then gratitude will well up within us to honor Him.

Gratitude makes us aware of the grace that has been imparted to us and will elevate us to see life from a different perspective—heights we have only dreamed of. When we are grateful, our attitude is positively affected and this enables us to handle adversity. When you begin to give thanks for what He has done and praise Him for what is about to happen, you open up the *"bottle of Gracerade"* and fill up your spirit (Ps. 100).

An attitude of gratitude determines our altitude. When everything seems to be falling apart, it may be God putting everything in place so that we can fulfill our destinies.

A great example of this is seen in the life of Hunter Williams, two-time team Captain of the Wake Forest University football team--an honor not often given to a player to be chosen by his teammates two years in a row! Especially to young man who was a walk-on and not heavily recruited out of high school.

At Wake Forest University, He was selected to the All-ACC Academic team two years in a row and a semi-finalist for the Burlsworth Trophy. This award is given annually to the most outstanding football player in America who began his career as a walk-on.

At Wake Forest High School, Hunter was an impact player on and off the field-- National Honor Society, an All-Conference linebacker and Conference defensive player of the year. He led his team to a state championship finals game his senior year. Unfortunately, no one came calling to recruit him to play at the next level. We prayed together about this dilemma. After much heart searching, Hunter believed that God wanted him to see that being His son was more important than being a college football player. He wanted Hunter to love Him even if football was no longer in his future. His identity and value was not in his ability to play football, but as a son in God's family. Just like Hunter, be a great man or woman who just so happens to be an athlete!

Eventually an opportunity was given to him to walk-on at WFU. Hunter lived out the seven winning plays for life and became a great example to his university, teammates, and his community. He became a well-rounded person, a "3-Dimensional" athlete. Hunter developed spiritually, mentally, and physically. He glorified God! He reflected God's character of excellence and not giving up. Hunter's career as a football player is now over, but his example and the lessons he learned can be shared for generations to come. He graduated with honors and has a promising future. We recently met for lunch and the joy that he displayed was genuinely contagious. Hunter will continue to be an impact player running the winning plays for life in the other arenas of business, relationships, and community. I praise God for his example!

Second Corinthians 2:14 says, "Thanks be to God who ALWAYS leads us in HIS triumph in Christ ...."

NOW it is your turn!

Take-Aways: Diesel Power

Definition: God's riches (enabling power) At Christ's expense

Fruit: Overcoming sustainable power through the Holy Spirit, victory, joy

1. Don't rely on your ability to behave in a particular way; instead, rely on God, who has the power to save (Ephesians 2:8–10, 1 Timothy 1:13–17, 1 Timothy 1:9).

2. Grace is the power that enables you to live out your destiny (1 Peter 5:10).

3. Grace is the premium gas in your game-changing vehicle for the journey.

4. Anything else is inferior and will eventually burn you out (Prov. 14:12, Titus 2:11–14).

5. My ability to extend grace towards others is strengthened by my gratitude to God for His unmerited blessings in my life.

6. Grace is the ultimate source to empower you (Heb. 4:16, 2 Peter 1:3–4).

7. Jesus is the giver of grace in abundance when and where you need it. Romans 5:17

If you daily choose to Diligently practice your Disciplines with Determination in God's divine Direction and power (Diesel) using Discernment, then you will have a great Destiny.

Let's Talk about Diesel Power- "Gracerade":

1. What do you rely on when you are looking for strength?

2. How do you motivate yourself?

3. How do you define grace?

4. What are some practical ways to activate His grace in your life?

5. What are you thankful for?

Winning Plays for Life

Let's Talk about Diesel Power Generators

1. What do you rely on when you are looking for a friend?

2. How do you choose?

What are the Benefits?

Chapter 8

MORE STORIES ON THE WINNING PLAYS FOR LIFE

(All stories written by A.J. Carr throughout the amazing 50 plus years of his reporting except for the last one written about him.)

And let us not grow weary of doing good, for in due season we will reap, if we do not give up ----Galatians 6:9

In his early seasons at Duke, before he became famous "Coach K," Mike Krzyzewski endured some hard times on the hardwood.

His first three Blue Devils teams went 37-48, which created a cauldron of discontent among Duke fans. Athletics director Tom Butters received more than 100 letters from supporters pleading for him to fire the young coach with the tongue-twisting name. Butters didn't budge. He stuck by his man and Krzyzewski figured out a successful recruiting formula, upgraded the talent level, and coached wisely. The result is an amazing winning record that includes more than 1,000 victories, most in NCAA Division I history.

"I think it's going to work out," Butters quipped years later of his decision to keep Krzyzewski.

Widely heralded as a premier leader, motivator and coach who astutely adapts to the ever-changing personnel and situations. Krzyzewski's accomplishments included five national championships, 12 Final Fours, 14 conference tournament titles and 3 straight Olympic Gold Medals through 2017.

That record also can be attributed to keen discernment, discipline and diligent preparation. Krzyzewski's teams are ready to play.

DIRECTION

A few miles down the road from rival Duke, Dean Smith also experienced trying times early in his tenure at North Carolina and was even hung in effigy. But a resilient Smith weathered the setbacks with determination, built a powerhouse program and developed the "System" that included multiple offenses, defenses and innovative ploys modeled by coaches at various levels. For the record, Smith retired with 17 regular season conference titles, 13 league tournament crowns, two National championships and 879 career victories, a record later surpassed by Bob Knight and Krzyzewski.

Legendary UCLA coach John Wooden, whose Bruins claimed 10 NCAA championships, expressed how he was amazed Smith's Carolina teams could successfully execute so many different schemes. Yet for all his basketball knowledge, and devotion to detail, a humble Smith never claimed to know it all.

Bill Lam, former UNC championship wrestling coach whose office was next to the Tar Heel legend's, saw Smith leaving Chapel Hill one day and asked him where he was going.

"To a clinic," Smith said.

"You are giving one?" Lam assumed.

"No." Smith went on to say he was going to observe and that if he could learn just one new thing, It would be worth his time and effort.

Both Smith and Kryzewski kept learning and consistently benefited from signing some of the nation's top talent. But as John Wooden pointed out, not all coaches who have outstanding talent win.

N.C. State's Norm Sloan was one who knew how to win with outstanding talent -- and with underdog players. In 1971 his Wolfpack shocked ACC regular season champion South Carolina in a slow tempo, low-scoring game to capture the conference tournament crown.

In 1974 Sloan's highly talented Pack went 30-1 and won the national championship, ending UCLA's seven-year reign. Sloan adjusted, loosened the reins, kept players relaxed and masterfully guided a unique team that featured the great David Thompson, towering Tommy Burleson and little Monte Towe.

Adhering to the philosophy "if you have a great player, let him play great," Sloan gave Thompson freedom to maximize his extraordinary talent in a fluid, free flowing offense rather than restrict him in tightly structured sets. Stars Burleson, Towe and the rest of the Pack also thrived with that offensive strategy.

UNC's Roy Williams is another coach who knows how to manage and succeed with top-notch players. He has had blue-chip talent at Kansas and North Carolina, claimed many titles at both schools, including three national crowns at UNC, and won around 80 percent of his games.

DIRECTION

Those who trust in the Lord will renew their strength. They will soar on wings like eagles; they will run and not grow weary, they will walk and not be faint – Isaiah 40:31

With a forty-four-inch vertical leap and exquisite basketball skills, David Thompson soared to super-stardom.

He was a two-time National Player of the Year who led NC State to the 1974 NCAA championship and became the top pick in the 1975 NBA draft. An all-around, all-court performer who excelled below the rim and above the rim, Thompson produced the deeds to equal his promise as a pro for several seasons with Denver.

He made All-Star teams, scored 73 points in one game, poured in 40 points or more 17 times, and at one juncture was the world's highest-paid athlete competing in a team sport. Then something went awry. Thompson lost his direction, succumbing to a rich social scene that led to drug and alcohol abuse. His performances declined. His marriage broke up for three years. He spent time in jail and rehab. "I felt lost," Thompson said in a *Raleigh News & Observer* story. "I thought, 'How

could I allow these things to happen—jail, ruined relationships, career?'
I was hurting."

It was during his brief time behind bars that Thompson, raised in a
Christian family in Shelby, N.C., rededicated his life to Christ. Moving
in the right direction again, he went from helpless to helpful. While
his illustrious pro basketball career was short-circuited by drugs, his
marriage, family life, and faith were restored. Humble and grateful,
Thompson has since shared with multitudes his rise-demise-rise-again
faith journey and how Christ redirected him to the real abundant life.
Credits: The News & Observer

DETERMINATION

He didn't have a nickname like "Tiger" or "Golden Bear," and he didn't
play on the PGA tour, but Charlie Boswell was one of sport's most
remarkable golfers. During an exhibition at Greensboro, NC, he awed
observers by belting accurate shot after shot onto the green. A coach
placed the ball, lined up his stance, and Boswell stroked it solidly.

It was an impressive feat for anyone, especially for a blind golfer.

According to the Alabama Tourism site, Boswell won 11 international
and 17 national blind golf titles. A former football and baseball player
at the University of Alabama, Boswell lost his vision while serving as an
infantry captain during World War II. After that devastating setback,
he took up golf and made an athletic comeback.

In addition to becoming the most renowned blind golfer in the country,
he helped raise lots of money for the Eye Foundation of Birmingham. All
that prompted famous comedian Bob Hope to call Boswell "America's
greatest inspiration."

For the Lord has not given us a spirit of fear, but of power, and of love and of a sound mind. – 2 Timothy 1:7

On the pitcher's mound, Jim "Catfish" Hunter never backed down. Didn't matter who the batter was, the team name on the opponent's jersey, or if the bases were loaded with nobody out.

Hunter was farm-boy strong with the confidence, determination and competitive ferocity of a boxing champion. Asked how he felt in intense pressure situations, Hunter gave a quick-pitch answer: "I feel like the pressure is on the batter."

Catfish.

It was a catchy nickname reportedly penned on him by Oakland A's owner Charles Finley, who gave the prize pitcher his first big contract. More important than the enduring nickname, Catfish flashed a Hall of Fame game.

In a 15-year career he posted a 224-166 record, pitched a perfect game in 1968, was an eight-time All-Star, and played a major role on 5 World Series championship teams with the Oakland A's and New York Yankees. Along with his grit, Hunter was a control artist, nipping corners of the plate, moving the ball around, hitting the right spots.

"He was always in control and he could throw any pitch he had for a strike," said Clyde King, a former Big League pitcher who held multiple high positions in the majors.

While Hunter was a big-time pitcher, he remained a humble, small-town man who retired to his sprawling farm in Hertford, where he grew up working and playing ball. Hunter was a devoted husband, father of three children, and a solid citizen who helped his community in a variety of ways before stricken with Amoytrophic Lateral Selercosi, also known as Lou Gehrig's disease.

He died at age 53 after battling the illness much the way he pitched — with faith and fierce determination.

Iron sharpens iron, and one man sharpens another – Proverbs 27:17

John Isner could have wilted on Wimbledon's grass court.

Instead, with an unbelievable will that perhaps even exceeded his considerable skill, Isner gutted it out and left a lasting mark in tennis lore during a 2010 marathon match. It was the longest duel in the sport's history, lasting 11 hours and 5 minutes spanning three interrupted, nerve-wracking days. At last Isner, a Greensboro N.C. native, finally edged gritty and determined Nicolas Mahut in the fifth and decisive set, 70-68.

It all started at 6:13 p.m. on a Tuesday and finished two days later --on a Thursday at 4:47 p.m. --when Isner closed with a crackling forehand winner. During that match Isner slammed 112 aces to Mahut's 103, and boomed 246 winners to Mahut's 244. So Isner gained fame by enduring and winning. Yet after the memorable Wimbledon moment, he was quoted in an Associated Press story that he didn't want that match to "define my career."

Isner felt he could accomplish more. A four-time college All-America at Georgia, Isner attained a No. 1 U.S. pro ranking, earned a top10 world ranking, and had won 10 tour titles through 2015. Like many other athletes, Isner used his sport and celebrity status to host a tennis charity that generated funds for cancer research.

At 6-10, he looks like a basketball player, a game he also enjoyed.

But when it came time to specialize, Isner focused on tennis. By the looks of it, he chose the right sport and right court.

Therefore I run in such a way, as not without aim; I box in such a way, as not beating the air – 1 Corinthians 9:26

During a brief interview with Rocky Marciano in the 1960s, I asked him if he could beat loquacious heavyweight boxing champion Cassius Clay, who later became known as Muhammad Ali. Replying as quickly as he could throw a knockout punch, Marciano emphatically said: "I could beat him." No doubt. No question.

Then retired, Marciano was still the personification of confidence and determination as a fighter. Those traits, along with his sharp boxing skills, were some of the reasons he compiled a perfect record during his reign as heavyweight champion between 1952 and 1956.

DILIGENCE

The plans of the diligent lead surely to advantage…Proverbs 21:5a

He had the streamlined look and sure hands of a gifted receiver, and from 1955 to 1967, that's what Raymond Berry was for the Baltimore Colts. He caught 631 passes—then an NFL record—for 9,275 yards, figures that earned him a place in Pro Football's Hall of Fame. Not bad for a player who wasn't the biggest or strongest but who arguably worked the hardest to perfect his craft.

"I could always catch the ball," Berry once shared when in Raleigh, NC to speak at a Fellowship of Christian Athletes function. Still, he added: "I had to work for every edge I could find. Receivers would break their fingers. I worked with putty, got them hard so I wouldn't get hurt. I figured there were eighteen different kinds of catches you could make. I set up drills and caught a hundred balls every day, making all the different kinds of catches."

Fabled quarterback Johnny Unitas passed and Berry caught, and once the ball was in Berry's hands, it was as secure as if it were in an armored car. He fumbled only once in thirteen NFL seasons.

"I had a bad experience fumbling in college, so I made a conscious effort never to fumble again," Berry explained. "I learned to put my fingers over the tip of the ball, tuck it in my rib cage, and protect it with both hands." Berry was always more than a dedicated player: he was anchored to a deep faith. He used to tape Bible verses above his locker and has shared his Christian beliefs throughout the country.

"God is moving among athletes," Berry said. "Athletes have a platform. I think the [Christian] influence of athletes has vastly increased over the last [several decades]."

Credits: The News & Observer

DILIGENTLY PRACTICING DISCIPLINES

In all toil there is profit, but mere talk tends only to poverty— Proverbs 14:23

As former Virginia Tech basketball star Erik Green will no doubt attest, the off-season is a big season, the time when a player can take his game to a higher level. So during the summer prior to his senior year, the Hokies' guard embarked on a workout regimen that mandated he make at least 20,000 shots.

Green spent hours in the gym, sweating and swishing basket after basket, polishing his form, elevating his game. When school started, he followed a rise-and-shine routine, often getting in 300 shots before going to class.

That diligence and discipline, combined with his God-given touch, made a difference—a big difference. Green, who had scored 15.6 points per game as a junior, averaged 25 points his senior season, won the NCAA's Division I scoring title and likely kept Hokies fans doing the Hokey Pokey.

He was the player opponents focused on stopping, but didn't. Green kept scoring with a variety of moves and shots and was voted ACC Player of the Year, an award he probably never dreamed he'd win a year earlier.

No doubt, his diligence made a difference.

Millions of sports fans saw Mia Hamm display her world-class soccer skills, score goals, make big plays, win championships.

What most didn't see was the sweat behind the success, the effort she gave when coaches were not looking and no fans were cheering.

…"While everyone goes to practice, not everyone is putting in the extra hours," Hamm noted in her book, "Go For Goal, by Harper Collins Publishing. "This is what sets champions apart. They do what it takes no matter how painful, how boring, or how difficult it is to find the time."

Hamm sparked North Carolina to four of the 22 national titles under heralded coach Anson Dorrance and set Atlantic Coast Conference records for most goals, assists and total points.

Then she starred on National Teams, helping the U.S. win 2 World Cups, 2 Olympic Gold Medals and set a record for most international goals, a mark that stood until 2013.

Unlike many of his basketball peers, Phil Ford "couldn't" dunk. That athletic shortcoming led to an inspiring children's book titled "The Kid Who Couldn't Dunk" featuring Ford and written by noted long-time writer Art Chanksy.

"I never could (really) dunk," said Ford, who added that he did manage to barely squeeze the ball over the rim one time at a pep rally.

As a 6-2 point guard Ford worked diligently to develop multiple skills, played below the rim and dazzled opponents of all sizes --including dunking dudes-- with his shake and bake moves, ball-handling wizardry and scoring ability. At the University of North Carolina, he won a 1978 National College Player of the Year award and was a three-time All-America who scored more than 2,000 points and dished out over 600 assists.

In 2012 Ford was inducted into the College Basketball Hall of Fame.

He also played six seasons in the NBA and earned a Rookie of the Year award before becoming an assistant coach at UNC and then in the pros. In college Ford flourished under the astute guidance of iconic coach Dean Smith.

A faithful Christian, Ford most importantly follows the guidance of his Heavenly Coach and God's Word, particularly drawing strength from Proverbs 3:5: "Trust in the Lord with all your heart and lean not on your own understanding..."

"When things are going bad that helps put things in perspective," Ford said. "I'm a child of God, try to do right and treat everybody right."

These days Ford trains aspiring young basketball players at a Raleigh, N.C. training facility, fittingly named Pro 3:5 Sports. He also developed a charity foundation that supports the effort to combat childhood obesity.

In short, "The Kid Who Couldn't Dunk" has the spunk, skill and will to still contribute much on and off the court.

The 2016 Olympic flame has flickered out, but the golden performances of gymnast wonder Simone Biles sparkle in memory.

At age 19, the smiling, springy 5-4 Biles won 4 individual gold medals and a silver while leading the U.S. to victory.

Much of her success can be traced to a disciplined training program she followed with great diligence. For a long time prior to the games, Biles trained six days a week and a total of 32 hours.

According to blog.gkelite.com, she toiled from 9 a.m. to 12 noon and 3 p.m. to 6 p.m. three days, from 12:30 p.m. to 5:30 p.m. two days during the week and from 9 am to 1 p.m. on Saturday. Sure, she also had skill, but without the will to follow that kind of rigorous regimen Biles probably wouldn't have become one of the Olympics' "Gold-en Girls.

Early in his freshman year at Duke, Shane Battier confided that he wasn't fond of the Blue Devils' conditioning program.

"I hate the conditioning," he told upper classman Steve Wojciechowski one day.

"'I hate losing,'" Wojo shot back, according to Battier.

That response triggered a change in Battier's attitude toward conditioning. "It was a key moment," he said during his speech on the night of his induction into Duke's Sports Hall of Fame. Battier embraced the fitness workouts along with Wojo and became one of the most dedicated, disciplined, diligent, elite players and leaders in Duke's storied basketball history.

Willing to assume whatever role it took to help his team win, Battier was a National Player of the Year, three-time National Defensive Player of the Year, All-Americam, Academic All-American and star on the 2001 NCAA championship team. Naturally, he was a favorite of the Cameron Crazies, who unleashed the enduring chant of "Who's Your Daddy?...Battier!.. Battier!"

Later, combining his multiple skills with an arduous work ethic, Battier played 15 years in the NBA and contributed to two world title teams with the Miami Heat.

Wojo was a scrappy, heady point guard and a basketball bandit who made lots of steals, and won lots of games. He helped the Blue Devils claim an ACC regular season title and earned a National Defensive Player of the Year honor during his career. As an assistant on Mike Krzyzewski's staff, Wojo had a hand in two Duke national titles — 2001 and 2010 — and in 2014 became the head coach at Marquette.

Battier and Wojo; Champions who worked hard and hated to lose.

Credit: GoDuke.com, Wikipedia

DISCIPLINE

Devote yourselves to prayer, being watchful and thankful –Colossians 4:2

The men's basketball locker room at Barton College, home of the 2007 NCAA Division II champions, was a small, crowded cubicle bearing the pungent scent of sweat.

For Coach Ron Lievense it's also a sanctuary, a place to meditate, read scripture, and pray. Several times during the week, he stands in front of each locker and prays for the player whose name is taped above the door. He asks God to help the athletes with personal needs and to grow spiritually as well as athletically.

"I want my players to understand I care for them," said Lievense, an All-America player who led Northwestern-St. Paul to the National Christian College basketball Championship in 1979-80. "I push them hard. I try to help them get better. But more importantly, I want them to know I pray for them and would help them in spiritual things as well. [This profession] is about things far greater than winning and losing, though you have to win to keep your job."

Lievense has had big wins and big seasons at Barton. His teams have captured multiple titles, including an incredible march to the national championship in 2007. That year Barton won all nine of its overtime games on the way to a 31–5 record, capped with a David-over-Goliath comeback. Down 7 points with less than a minute left in the title game, Anthony Atkinson scored 10 points in 45 seconds,, including the decisive basket that ended Winona State's 57-game winning streak.

Born into a Christian home, Lievense says it's still challenging to keep from stumbling in the emotional, pressurized climate of college basketball. "It's a day-to-day struggle, especially in heated competition, with the expectation level, my own weaknesses, and the pressure on myself to be successful," he said. "There are times I'm too hard on my team [and] times I'm too hard on the officials. I want to win. I pray to keep that balance, for God to do with me as he sees fit so I can be a positive example and not shame the Kingdom [with] my behavior."

To stay strong, Lievense settles in his office on game days and reads from a stack of about fifty Bible verses he has handwritten on well-worn index cards. When he prays for his players, he lifts up specific issues but always prays they will realize the "need to seek the Lord with all their heart, soul, and mind and look for a relationship with Him."

Credit: The News & Observer

DISCERNMENT

Blessed is the one who finds wisdom, and the one who gets understanding.

Proverbs 3:13

Growing up in Goldsboro, North Carolina, Dave Odom fervently followed Atlantic Coast Conference basketball. He saw successful coaches like N.C. State's Everett Case, Wake Forest's Bones McKinney, Duke's Hal Bradley, and North Carolina's Frank McGuire. He admired the galaxy of stars such as State's Ronnie Shavlik, Carolina's Lennie Rosenbluth, Wake Forest's Len Chappell and Duke's Dick Groat.

Years later, notably in 1995 and 1996, thousands of fans were admiring Odom on the ACC's center stage. He was guiding Wake Forest to two straight conference tournament championships, which hadn't happened at Wake in more than three decades.

Reaching that pinnacle wasn't easy. Odom faced a colossal challenge when he took over the Deacons' program in 1989.

Wake was deep in the doldrums after four straight losing seasons. The Deacons needed a spark and more talent. It was a daunting task for the small Atlantic Coast Conference school to sign the most elite prospects established powers Duke and North Carolina pursued.

Odom assessed the situation and devised a recruiting plan. While looking for top talent, he had to find players who weren't caught up in the tradition of Wake's in-state rivals. He and his staff also had to sharply evaluate prospects and identify some players who were not the most highly rated, but could develop with good coaching.

His recruiting pitch was "You Can Be Difference Makers" at Wake Forest.

A breakthrough came with the signing of McDonald's All-America Rodney Rogers from Durham who became an ACC Player of the Year and went on to a productive NBA career.

Odom, a former two-sport Athlete of the Year winner at Guilford College, later added Tim Duncan from the Virgin Islands and found guard Randolph Childress in the Winston-Salem area.

Duncan, who burgeoned into an All-American and became a 15-time All-Pro for the San Antonio Spurs. and Childress, a high-scoring guard, played major roles on those two title teams. Prior to that championship run in the 1990s, Wake had won only two ACC tournaments since the ACC was formed in 1953.

Without discernment, sound teaching and coaching, Odom likely wouldn't have led Wake to 11 winning seasons in 12 years, the two ACC titles, eight NCAA playoff appearances and earned three Conference Coach of the Year honors.

Terry Holland, like his friend and former assistant Odom, was not afraid to tackle a challenge.

A former star and successful coach at Davidson, Holland stepped into a "Basketball Graveyard" at UVA. Prior to his arrival in '74 the Cavaliers had won just 39 percent of their games in the previous 17 seasons.

Holland turned the program around with solid coaching and strong recruiting that included signing heralded Ralph Sampson, who became a 3-time National Player of the Year. In 16 years Holland's UVA teams compiled a 326-173 record, won the school's first ACC Tournament, one NIT title, went to 2 Final Fours and 9 NCAA playoffs.

During his glory days on Vic Bubas' powerhouse Duke teams, Jeff Mullins made an indelible mark as a high-scoring, two-time All-America forward. But when he joined the NBA St. Louis Hawks, it was different. At the behest of his coach, Mullins switched to guard behind two veterans whose style and mindset was drive to the basket and shoot old-fashioned set shots.

Mullins was a jump shooter who didn't fit the drive-and set-shot system. It was adjust or bust—until Bill Sharman intervened.

Sharman was a former star guard on the Boston Celtics dynasty teams with the gift of discernment. He had watched Mullins in St. Louis and after becoming the head coach at San Francisco -- now Golden State - initiated a trade that brought the young NBA player to the Warriors.

Sharman's succinct instruction was "run the floor and play like you did at Duke," Mullins recalled.

Mullins, one of the game's finest gentlemen, became a three-time All-Star and helped the Warriors capture a NBA championship during his distinguished 10-year career.

DESTINY – WINNING PLAYS FOR LIFE IN ACTION!

My sheep listen to my voice; I know them, and they follow me.

—John 10:27-28

Like an Old Testament prophet, Danny Lotz said he was jolted awake in the middle of the night by a heavenly voice.

At a 2007 Fellowship of Christian Athletes conference in Black Mountain, NC, Lotz, who was a long-time Raleigh Bible Study leader, said he heard God speaking to him at 2 a.m.

"The call was so clear," Lotz explained. "He said: 'Dan, here are two athletes, two old men, but what are you and Albert doing for the University of North Carolina?'" Moments later, Lotz, then 70 years old, awakened his 75-year old camp roommate and long-time friend, Albert Long, and told him "we've got to pray right now" about starting a Bible study at UNC-Chapel Hill, where both men had gained athletic fame.

"I thought he was having a nightmare," Long said. "He woke me up three times, and I'd say: 'Let's talk about it tomorrow, Danny!'"

But Lotz insisted on praying then and there. A few days later they were making arrangements to start a weekly men's Bible study at their alma mater.

Eight men came to the first meeting. Since then the group has grown to well over 50. Coaches former athletes, faculty members and residents have gathered to eat, pray, read scripture, and listen to messages by Long, Lotz, and more recently, other speakers.

"It has been wonderful and it's open to all adults," said Long, a Durham native who founded and led Happenings, Inc., a Christian youth ministry, for decades (25 years). "Our whole objective is to teach the word of God."

Both men lived out Psalm 71:18: "Even when I am old and gray, do not forsake me, O God, until I declare your power to the next generation, and Your might to all who are to come."

For Lotz and Long, that also meant visiting coaches and leading a weekly study for UNC's Fellowship of Christian Athletes chapter, which Lotz started while a student in 1958. Since then each man has been selected to the FCA's national Wall of Fame for their long, devoted service to the ministry.

Lotz, who died in 2015, was a dentist by profession, heralded as a player on UNC's 1957 National Championship basketball team and widely known as a Bible teacher and spiritual leader.

The son of a minister and son-in-law of evangelist Billy Graham, Lotz was a 6-foot-7 gentle giant, spoke with a soft voice, walked with a deliberate gait, and possessed a quick wit that put people at ease in group settings.

Long is trim and fit, 6-feet tall, effusive and exudes as much or more enthusiasm than famed football coach Lou Holtz giving a pep talk. Like Holtz, he speaks with machine-gun rapidity, which once prompted former Duke basketball coach Bucky Waters to call him the "fastest talking man" in North Carolina.

Long used that salesman delivery to develop a lucrative insurance business. But his life changed when Danny and brother John Lotz took him to an FCA conference in New York in the 1950s. After that spiritual awakening, Long started Happenings, Inc, and shared the gospel at more than 2,000 youth assemblies and churches throughout the southeast.

Long had a platform that appealed to audiences, having been the Atlantic Coast Conference's only four-sport letterman — competing in football, basketball, baseball and track at UNC. Young and old alike respond to the man and his message.

"Albert is one of the most infectious people I've ever met," said Doug Shackleford, professor at UNC's Kenan-Flagler Business School. He also said, "Danny is one of the most Godly, soft-hearted people I've met. When he speaks, it's like E.F. Hutton — everybody listens."

When God spoke, Danny listened, and as a result multitudes have been blessed.

Partial Reprint from 2007 story in The News & Observer

Let each of you look not only to his own interests, but also to the interests of others – Philippians 2:4

When Davis Lee prepared to tee off at Wallace, N.C.'s River Landing golf course one day in 2013, M.L. Carr walked up wearing ragged old jeans, a T-shirt and scruffy sneakers and asked if he could caddy for the older man. In that un-golf attire, Carr, a former Boston Celtic basketball player, was re-creating a scene from 50 years earlier when he had approached Lee at Wallace's Rockfish Country Club and asked about carrying his bag.

"Son, do you know anything about caddying?" Lee asked the teenager that day.

"No, but I'll do it a month for free if you'll teach me," Carr offered.

"With your attitude and my billfold, we can make a good partnership," Lee quipped.

That was the beginning of what Carr calls a *real* "Blind Side" story, drawing on the movie by that title. The Hollywood version showed how Sean and Leigh Ann Tuohy took in a desperate African American youth, Michael Oher, gave him a good home and put him on track toward a college education and successful NFL career that included stints with the Baltimore Ravens and Carolina Panthers.

In the Duplin County "Blind Side," Lee, who is white, took a special interest in Carr, an African American, and steered him like a father would on a course that led to basketball and business success. Carr starred at Wallace-Rose Hill High, was an All-America on Guilford College's 1973 National NAIA championship team, then had a rewarding career in the NBA as a player and front office executive.

"I had a great family. My mother and father were outstanding people," Carr said. "{But} If it hadn't been for Davis, this {success} wouldn't have happened, none of it. I don't know which direction I would have gone." That's why Carr honored his long time mentor, friend and business partner with a surprise celebration at River Landing.

"I don't know why Davis had an interest in me; it wasn't a popular thing to do in the '60s," Carr said, recalling the country's turbulent racial unrest in that era. "But I've seen him help people from all different backgrounds. He has a heart bigger than his body."

The men work together at Davis Lee Companies, headquartered in Huntsville, Ala. The diverse businesses include three poultry processing plants, Dream Insurance, Liberty Legacy, Lee Energy, Fort Payne Wholesale, and L-Sync. Dream Insurance, in which Carr is heavily involved, offers affordable coverage for low-income families. Liberty Legacy provides a program for teachers to promote patriotism in schools, something especially important to Lee.

"It all germinated with Davis saying 'you can caddy for me' and convincing me to go to Wallace-Rose Hill," said Carr, acutely aware of how one caring, nurturing, benevolent man can make an impact in another's life. One day Carr asked what he could do to repay Lee for his kindness.

"Help another kid," Lee said.

Taking that answer to heart, Carr has helped and inspired many young and old, as a star athlete, by writing books, speaking and creating three charity foundations.

DIESEL – "GRACERADE"

All things work together for those who love the Lord and are called according to His purpose – Romans 8:28

Dexter Williams' basketball dream was dying. For the second straight year, the ebullient, hopeful senior guard wasn't picked to play on Raleigh Enloe High's varsity. It was a painful cut and the depth of his disappointment was unmeasurable.

Then God sent an "angel" to Williams' home one day. He was Coach Jack Hawke, a noted North Carolina politician who consoled and encouraged the teenager, and invited him to play on his Boys and Girls Club travel team.

"God used {Coach Hawke} to keep my dream going and that's why I am so adamant now about helping kids," said Williams, who has spent years coaching and training young basketball players with a Christian perspective. While playing Williams also got the attention of a former college player, Jack Jackson, who helped him get a scholarship at Clinton Junior College.

Seizing this unexpected opportunity, Williams blossomed into a model student-athlete, a two-time basketball All-America and two-time Academic All-America at Clinton. Armed with success and brimming with renewed confidence, he went on to Hampton University, where he set three-point shooting records. After that Williams played several years on various traveling teams, among them Athletes in Action and the Globetrotter Legends.

A Legend. Pretty good for a kid who never made his high school varsity team. But maybe Williams was born to be a Globetrotter, a showman as well as a basketball craftsman. "When I was seven years old I dreamed I saw Jesus," he said. "I didn't see his face. {But} He handed me a red, white and blue basketball."

The color of the Globetrotters' basketball.

Williams dazzled massive crowds with a Trotter's, vivacious personality, and his lovable monitor, "Love Boat."

He chose that nickname for himself, explaining: "I love people and I want them to see the love of Christ in me…(Traveling around) I wanted to give them a boat load of the love of Christ."

Williams, who initially spent "9 or 10" hours daily developing his Trotter tricks, has staged mesmerizing ball handling shows around the world and delivered his Christian message to multitudes, young and old. Everywhere, people love the "Love Boat," who is still afloat on the court and in his faith.

A former successful high school coach in Carteret County (NC), Williams' focus now is teaching young players basketball skills, directing summer camps with wife Shannon, following his four sons' games, and sharing the gospel.

"I'm grateful," Williams said. "God worked everything out."

DESTINY

Growing up in Philadelphia, Lou Pucillo experienced disappointment much like Williams.

He did make his high school team, but never was a starter. Yet little Lou (5-9) soared from high school sub to college All-American. Overlooked by scouts, Pucillo continued playing in the Philly area and caught the eye of then keen observing NC State assistant Vic Bubas with his magician-like ball handling and passing skill.

When Bubas suggested giving the 5-9 guard a scholarship, reluctant head coach Everett Case questioned his assistant's sanity. But Bubas, a masterful recruiter who could spot talent in the dark, convinced Case to sign Pucillo. The result: State got a "Lou Lou" of a player who dazzled opponents and had Wolfpack fans howling with delight.

Pucillo blossomed into a First Team All-America, claimed an ACC Athlete of the Year award, and helped lead State to the ACC tournament title in1959.

WINNING PLAYS FOR LIFE IN ACTION

(There) is a time to weep, and a time to laugh, a time to mourn, and a time to dance...Ecclesiastes 3:13

Amid the euphoric Carolina Hurricanes' 2006 Stanley Cup celebration, there was Rod Brind' Amour with the treasured trophy hoisted above his head. It was the captain's crowning moment, the only significant piece that had been missing from his sparkling National Hockey League resume.

"At my age (then 35} there was nothing left but to win," Brind'Amour said. "It was almost surreal...something you dreamed about your whole life. I felt so fulfilled." While winning the Cup is the desired destination of players and teams, getting there is no easy skate around the ice.

"It didn't just happen," Brind'Amour reflected. "It takes discipline, diligence, all the people you did it with. It's not an individual award. It's such a journey of every day doing the right things."

The journey is long, arduous, grinding. But Brind'Amour always had an affinity for training as well as the will and skill to win. When playing at Michigan State, he was known as "Rod The Bod" for his physical fitness and fanatical workouts. It was a quality he carried into the NHL and sustained for 21 years.

While playing for the Hurricanes, there were days in June that he would be in Raleigh's PNC Arena, running stadium steps alone, "almost dying," with nobody in the stands, nobody cheering. Yet a sweating Brind'Amour believed "it's gonna pay off."

It did and the extra effort, the grueling workouts, were worth it.

In the 'Canes' Stanley Cup run, Brind Amour scored 12 goals, tops among playoff players, and his competitive fervor rather than pep talks inspired talented teammates.

Overall, Brind'Amour totaled 452 career goals, 1,184 points, 732 assists, made the 1992 All-Star team, and won 2 Selke trophies — an award given to the NHL forward who best excels on defense. And he helped his team win that coveted Stanley Cup.

Through it all, the triumphs and trials, it's was a strong faith that has and continues to sustain him.

"I have God in my life," said Brind' Amour, who reads the Bible regularly. "I have had a lot of ups and downs in my career and life. I know that {God} is always with me. I'm not by myself. It's a powerful thing."

DIRECTION – DETERMINATION –
DESTINY – GRACERADE

"I BELIEVE"

In the beginning, there were plenty of skeptics. They didn't envision East Carolina's 1991 Pirates creating a national ripple in the college football world. Once again ECU appeared over-scheduled and undermanned, an old refrain heard so many times in the past.

Then the Pirates kicked off the season at Illinois, fell behind, rallied, suffered from a crucial call Big Ten officials later admitted was wrong and lost 38-31. Yet that defeat might have been a turning point, Coach Bill Lewis said. After that defeat, the Pirates exuded renewed confidence, determination, an "I Believe" attitude, and some unbelievable things began to happen.

Opponents that had been unbeatable in previous seasons succumbed to the Pirates. South Carolina fell. So did Syracuse and Pittsburgh. Lewis rode off the field on his players' shoulders. Goal posts came down in purple-clad celebrations. Fans filled Ficklen Stadium and hopped on the ECU bandwagon.

Following that season-opening defeat, ECU reeled off 11 straight victories — after trailing in eight of those games. The Pirates gained a final No. 9 national ranking, and capped the best record in school history (11-1) with a dramatic 37-34 comeback win over N.C. State in the Peach Bowl. Along the way they listened to lyrics from a Kenny Rogers' song, "when you put your heart in it, it'll take you anywhere," and the Pirates played to that upbeat tune.

They had the heart of a champion, they had the talent, and they had the coaching.

Quarterback Jeff Blake, a prolific passer tutored by co-offensive coordinator Steve Logan, threw for more than 3,000 yards and led a high-octane offense. Robert Jones performed like an All-America linebacker, which he was, and anchored the defense. Both Pirate standouts later played in the NFL. With Blake, Jones, (and) talented, hard-nosed and mentally tough teammates, the Pirates executed the team's "I Believe" theme to the hilt in the memorable Peach Bowl.

With 8:41 remaining, they trailed 34-17. But Blake still believed and was brilliant in the clutch. He completed 15 of 21 passes on three scintillating scoring drives and delivered the game-winning toss to tight end Luke Fisher with 1:32 left. Meanwhile, the defense dug down and came up with three straight stops in the fourth quarter. Through it all, this team taught us unforgettable lessons about how to cope with adversity, about never giving up, about believing when others doubted.

PIRATES PRAYER
BY C.B. OWENS, TEAM CHAPLAIN

Our Father, I thank you for demonstrating your belief in me by endowing me with the gifts and talents to be an athlete.

I thank you for my parents, friends and coaches who have throughout the years showed their belief in me, disciplining and encouraging me to be the best I could be. I thank you for East Carolina University believing in me enough to give me an opportunity to get an education and at the same time use my talents to play the game of football.

I thank you for Coach Bill Lewis, his coaching staff, and the rest of the Pirate support staff for their belief in me and showing me how to believe in you and my teammates.

I also thank you for Pirate fans, who believed in us when we were 0-1 and encouraged us along the difficult road of being 11-1 with their slashing sabers and chants of "We Believe."

Together, we have learned the rewards are great for those who believe and work hard. The greatest reward I have received because of everyone's belief in me is that I am able to believe in myself.

Father, help us all to continue to believe in each other and to take that belief to a higher level as we believe in you and receive the greatest gift of all —ETERNAL LIFE.

In the name and power of Jesus Christ, I believe (John 3:16).

Amen

With God's help we will do mighty things," Psalm 60:12

George Williams was a basketball man, a former All-Conference player at St. Augustine's College, then an assistant coach at his alma mater. "I wanted to be a basketball coach," Williams said, but his career path changed in 1976 when a school official asked him to add "interim" track coach to his duties.

Interim turned into permanent. Nearly four decades later Williams was still on the track, still traveling in the fast lane, still winning championships, the destination all teams strive to reach.

Through 2017 his St. Aug's teams had won 39 Division II national championships, the most among NCAA schools at all levels. Add to that over 160 CIAA titles, multiple individual champs, plus a 95-percent graduation rate.

"Academics, athletics, and a controlled social life," said Williams, citing priorities he set for his athletes to help keep them on the right track.

Williams's incredible resume also includes head coach of the 2004 U.S. Olympic team, coach of numerous Olympians and three gold medal winners, and induction into 8 Halls of Fame.

Williams is a man of faith who realizes his help comes from the Lord. He says reading verses from the Bible "keep me going," stresses that "God is in control" and knows the best crown of all, the most treasured destiny, is in the future.

DIRECTION

In their hearts humans plan their course, but the LORD establishes their steps

Proverbs 16:9

After a sparkling high school career as a defensive end, Jim Ritcher envisioned excelling at that same position when he arrived at N.C. State University. Sacking quarterbacks and racking up running backs with helmet-rattling tackles was his M O (Mode of Operation).

But Ritcher was blind-sided at his first college practice when Wolfpack coach Bo Rein told him to play *center.*

"I said, 'No, I don't want to do that.' I was about in tears," Ritcher recalled. "I thought that's where you put your little sister playing backyard football. I wanted to play *football...*" hard tackling, smash-mouth football.

While Ritcher resisted, Rein persisted. At first the rookie had trouble simply snapping the ball. To make matters worse, senior nose tackle A. W. Jenkins kept beating him up in practice.

"Just let me play defense," Ritcher pleaded, but to no avail. Rein stuck with his decision and it proved to be the right decision.

Toward the end of his freshman season, Ritcher was the starting Pack center and on his way to stardom. His blend of strength and speed, plus a penchant for popping, enabled him to fire out from the line quickly and block linebackers as well as defensive linemen.

"His talent enabled us to outline certain plays we wouldn't have considered with normal players. He would be a star at any position other than quarterback or wide receiver." said Rein, who was quoted on the College Football Hall of Fame website.Typical of him, Ritcher deflected praise to his teammates. "I was honored, but it wasn't just me," he said. "We had really good teams, so many great players who didn't get recognized. Like the Bible says, we are all part of a body and one part is not more important than another."

Despite his modesty, Ritcher was something special, an All-American and winner of the 1980 Outland Trophy, which is presented to college football's top interior offensive lineman.

After graduating from State and shuffling off to Buffalo as a top draft choice in 1980, Ritcher seemed prepared for a pro career at center. However, after one season of snapping, the Bills moved him to guard, where he could better utilize his speed and quickness. He was adept at trap blocking and on end sweeps and a player coaches could count on as surely as they could depend on snowstorms in the winter. He was durable, diligent, disciplined, and played in two Pro Bowls and four Super Bowls with Buffalo, where he spent fourteen of his sixteen NFL seasons.

The Bills didn't win any of those Super Bowls, but they might have if there had been a few more Ritchers on the roster. "He may be the best athlete among offensive linemen I ever coached," coach Marv Levy told the *Raleigh News & Observer*. "He may be the best pulling lineman I ever had to lead a sweep, and he was maybe the best-conditioned athlete I had. He had great values, was clean living, and was by far one of the most respected players I ever coached."

Ritcher also had another passion and gift -- flying. Post NFL he became a long time commercial airlines pilot making international flights. Back on the ground and reflecting on his resistance about changing positions, Ritcher's thankful his perceptive coaches redirected him. He figures the move to center at State and switch to guard in Buffalo helped prolong and enhance his sterling career... enabled him to reach a special football destination.

There was more to it, he added.

"God was behind the scenes, working things out," said Ritcher, a family man with a wife and three athletic sons, and a man of profound faith.

Credit: GoPack.com

"Whatever you do, work at it with all your heart, as working for the Lord, not for human masters. " Colossians 3:23

A Helmet-Cracking Linebacker

Amid the multiple mementos and awards in Pat Teague's collection sits a cracked NC State football helmet. That battered old headgear is one of his most treasured trophies, one that jars memories of a collision in the 1980s with Maryland star running back Rick Badanjek. Teague was dazed by that smash up, yet he won the head-to-head battle, stopping the tough Terp on a key short-yardage down.

The heady hit also revealed much about how the aggressive 6'–2", 230-pound NC State linebacker played: with pop and passion. Teague was a leader of the 'Pack, a defensive standout, and a human tackling machine.

As a senior in 1986, he led NC State in stops with 128 stops, including a school record 26 tackles against Virginia Tech and 29 "unofficial" hits in a 35–34 win over rival North Carolina.

"He was one of best leaders and players I ever had the pleasure to coach," said Joe Pate, then NC State's defensive coordinator. "He was an example of what a student-athlete should be off the field as well as on the field. He's an all-around, All-American guy. As good as he was in football, he's an even better person."

Man on a Mission

Teague still has the look of a linebacker: Broad shoulders, strong arms, and sturdy legs that helped him stop ball carriers in the '80s. Since then his focus has widened. These days he's devoted to his wife, Sheila, and children, Brianna, Rachel, and Ethan. He is an engineer, has coached youth basketball, been an assistant for a high school football team, and remains active in Christian ministry.

After fourteen years as associate pastor at Raleigh's Covenant Church International, Teague founded and currently leads Sports Mission Outreach, ministering to high school and college athletes. Among those he has touched is the Wake Forest, N.C., High football team.

"You want young people to meet a person like Pat," said Wake High coach Reggie Lucas. "He's been an inspiration to our kids, and he's kept me on the right path, making sure my heart is in the right place. I appreciate that. He has a great understanding about athletes, (and emphasizes) you always want to be the best athlete and also be the best person."

Trials and Triumphs

Teague's athletic journey included four years at Raleigh's Sanderson High, where he was active in the Fellowship of Christian Athletes, competed in three-sports, and made prep football All-America. Scholarship offers from ACC schools and Tennessee enticed him, but he chose NC State after "much prayer and wise counsel."

However, at State he quickly discovered that college football was different than at Sanderson, where he was inducted into the high school's first Athletics Hall of Fame class.

He played for three Wolfpack head coaches—Monte Kiffin, Tom Reed, and Dick Sheridan—and had to adapt to several different defensive schemes. During that time he also grieved the sudden death of his father.

Leaning on his faith and receiving strong support from Coach Reed, Teague regrouped in time to play a reserve role behind starting linebackers Vaughan Johnson and Andy Hendel as a redshirt freshman. "I learned a lot from those guys," Teague said. "They set the tempo with their hitting. Vaughan and Andy were big hitters. They hustled every play. I knew you had to have a relentless attitude."

As a sophomore he cracked the starting lineup and was one of State's leading tacklers with 120 tackles. Then adversity struck and a disappointing junior year followed, triggered in part by a groin injury and a negative reaction to medication that sapped his strength.

Teague shouldered much of the blame for his demise as well, confessing, "That summer I did not train as hard. I strayed from the disciplines. It was a very good lesson to learn," albeit a painful one. When spring practice started, he still was not at full strength and "didn't impress [new] coach Dick Sheridan at all."

Prior to his senior year, Teague had to deal with personal demons: a fear of failure, facing the physical agony of extra off-season workouts, and the pressure of trying to regain starting status.

Recommitment

Teague trained sedulously in the mornings and after work. Eventually, he regained his direction, determination, discipline, and diligence.

"The whole summer was getting back to the basics, the joy of the game," Teague said. "I still had to convince the coaches I was good enough to start."

That wasn't easy, but by the season's third game Sheridan penciled him into the lineup. Once back, Teague played with tenacity leading the 'Pack with 154 tackles including the Peach Bowl. At season's end he received the Bob Warren Award for Integrity and Sportsmanship, the Mike Hardy Award for "playing beyond [his] capabilities" and was elected team captain by his teammates.

"I'm so grateful for my senior year," he said. "God gave me another opportunity."

All along, he drew strength from Proverbs 30:30: "Be like a mighty lion, who does not retreat before any."

Teague didn't retreat.

In addition to a twenty-six-tackle Peach Bowl performance against Virginia Tech and his twenty-nine hits against Carolina, he tamed Clemson's Tigers in 1986. His eleven tackles, six deflections, and one interception helped spark a 27–3 State rout in Carter-Finley Stadium.

It was "one of the greatest individual performances I've had the pleasure to see," Joe Pate said.

Teague heaped praise on Pate and linebacker coach Ken Pettus for helping him reach his potential. "Coach Pate had an amazing work ethic, set the bar where he expected you to be," he said. "Coach Pettus got me to play at that extra gear."

Teague, who spent two seasons in the NFL with Tampa Bay and a brief span with Cleveland before suffering a leg injury, still connects with his Wolfpack family and attends the players' annual reunion. "All my coaches and all my teammates enriched my life," said Teague, who enriched State football with his leadership, his character, and his helmet-cracking tackling.

Credit: GoPack.com

"You are our letter, written in our hearts, known and read by all men; being manifested that you are a letter of Christ, cared for by us, written not with ink but with the Spirit of the living God, not on tablets of stone but on tablets of human hearts." 2 Corinthians 3:2-3

(For the record I, Pat Teague insisted on this article on AJ to be inserted because he a great example of running the "Winning Plays for Life". He has been for over 50 years as a Brother in Christ, Husband, Father, Friend and Sports Writer.)

Courtesy of the The Raleigh News & Observer

By Chip Alexander

Staff Writer (Published in 2009)

Growing up in Wallace, in eastern North Carolina, A.J. Carr would read The News & Observer's sports pages in the early morning hours before leaving for school. In August 1966, he began working at The N&O, writing stories for the sports pages others wanted to get up early to read. Over the course of more than 40 years, that never changed, even if the newspaper, the industry and the sports he covered did.

And, say those who know him and have worked with him, A.J. Carr never changed. "A.J. is a one-of-a-kind 'throwback' in the best sense of the word," East Carolina athletic director Terry Holland said. "He has been able to thrive in a very different and more competitive world without losing his sense of humor or his graciousness."

Carr, 66, will retire from the newspaper next month. N&O senior vice president and executive editor John Drescher made the announcement on Thursday. "A.J. has been really good for a really long time," Drescher said. "I think he's just as good now as he's ever been. He understands the people who play so well. He writes about sports in very human terms. He's clearly held in high regard by his professional colleagues, the subjects of his stories and his sources."

Duke basketball coach Mike Krzyzewski once gave Carr a fist-bump on press row before a game at Cameron Indoor Stadium. If that has happened with any other writer, no one can recall it. "I've loved my association with A.J., and I can't think of any coach from any school in any sport who would not say the same thing," Krzyzewski said. "Because A.J. was trustworthy. You knew you could tell him anything, and he would say it exactly the way you wanted. He was never trying to trick you. "When you talk about honest, trustworthy and good, A.J.'s picture comes up."

The late Norman Sloan, who often had a tempestuous relationship with the media while N.C. State's basketball coach, once told a group of sportswriters: "If it wasn't for A.J. Carr of The News & Observer, I could say I hated every one of you sons of [guns]." Sloan's language was more colorful than that, but the point was made. Carr was an exception -- and exceptional. Carr deflects such praise. A quiet, gentle type who rarely raises his voice, a deeply religious man who never is profane, he said he felt "blessed and fortunate" to have worked for The

N&O nearly all of his professional career. "I always wanted to work here," he said. "Once I got here, I never wanted to leave. This is where I wanted to be." Carr said the man who hired him, longtime N&O sports editor Dick Herbert, was a "genuine giant in the business" who was a dutiful mentor and helped nurture his career. So, too, was Joe Tiede, who succeeded Herbert as sports editor.

Carr said a conversation with legendary Duke football coach Wallace Wade many years ago left an indelible impression. Wade was talking about recruiting Ace Parker, who would be a big Blue Devils star, and how Wade told Parker to always remember that Duke would do a lot more for him than he would ever do for Duke. "It really made me think," Carr said. "And when I think of The News & Observer, it has done a lot more for me than I've ever done for the paper."

Carr has covered Final Fours and bowl games but said he has put just as much effort into writing about a small-college athlete or the Senior Games. He twice was voted North Carolina sportswriter of the year by the National Sportscasters and Sportswriters Association. The awards in 1978 and 2008 were a testament to his longevity but also to the richness of his career.

In the early days, Carr would hunker down with his typewriter, twirl his wedding band for a few moments in thought, then begin banging out a story. The computer age brought on a bigger challenge -- working with a laptop, wireless, blogging.

This basketball season, after N.C. State upset Wake Forest, Carr hunkered down with his iBook, twirled the band and then banged out this:

For a moment, let your imagination run rampant.

Picture the No. 10 ranked team in the ACC beating the No. 7 ranked team in the nation. Envision N.C. State guard Farnold Degand outscoring Wake Forest's player of the year candidate Jeff Teague. Close your eyes and see Brandon Costner going on a wild scoring spree.

Imagine it. All that and more happened Wednesday night at the raucous RBC Center, where the Wolfpack emerged from the depths of the conference to conquer Wake Forest 82-76.

"A.J. is a writer that cared about the teams and the players and the coaches he met," North Carolina basketball coach Roy Williams said. "He is a writer who was not interested in being controversial; he was interested in writing his story. He didn't come along in that age where the more controversial, the better the story."

Carr always could get the story. He's competitive. He knew whom to call and his calls were almost always returned.

ECU's Holland noted Carr was rarely scooped "since he knows everyone and none of us can lie to or mislead him, even when we know that it is in our self-interest to at least mislead him."

Carr's colleagues perhaps will miss him most -- his humor in the office or the press box, the welcoming smile, the words of encouragement and praise.

Few have shared a press box with Carr as often as N&O sports columnist Caulton Tudor.

"Like lots of their readers, sportswriters have heroes, too," Tudor said. "But contrary to some public opinion, our heroes usually aren't famous coaches, all-star quarterbacks and high-scoring basketball players.

"Our heroes are seldom seen and rarely saluted. A.J. Carr has long been and forever will be as high on my hero list as you get. The reasons for that are as numerous as A.J.'s lifetime in the business. But to sum it up in a few words, A.J. is a great newspaper person but an even better pure person.

"To those of us who have been fortunate enough to work with him, A.J., at maybe 5-foot-8, is an all-time giant."

WHAT THEY'RE SAYING ABOUT A.J. CARR

"The words that come to mind with A.J. are courteous, honesty, diligence, fairness, great humility and great pride. All those things are interwoven in his life."
-- Former Wake Forest and East Carolina basketball coach Dave Odom

"Some people don't know that A.J. was a tremendous athlete at Wallace-Rose Hill [High School]. He was a hard worker, team player, unselfish and a true sportsman, the same attributes that he carried into his professional life in sports writing."
-- Wendell Murphy of Rose Hill, a friend of Carr's for more than 50 years and former chairman of the N.C. State board of trustees

"A.J.'s a giant in the media industry. He's got such a caring attitude; he doesn't try to make up the story, he just writes the story. He writes it as well as anybody that I've known, and I've always enjoyed reading him, and I've always enjoyed being interviewed by him."
-- North Carolina athletics director Dick Baddour

"During my 26 years in college athletics administration, I never met a finer gentleman in the media arena than A.J. Carr. I'm glad I had the good fortune to work with him directly during my tenure at East Carolina. He is a special person."
-- Former ECU and Florida State athletics director Dave Hart

"When I sat down to talk to A.J., and this has been over 31 years, I always felt like I was not going to read something that was 180 degrees from what I said. As a coach, I had a great deal of respect that A.J. wanted to get the story, he wanted to write the story, and he had in his mind that he wasn't going to jump away from it to be more controversial."
-- UNC basketball coach Roy Williams

"A.J. and I worked a lot of games together, and he was always a pleasure to work with and be with. He's the most polite person I've ever known. He's a rare individual."
-- Former N&O sports editor Joe Tiede

"I consider him a great friend. When he had his hip replaced, I visited him in the Duke hospital. And so I have two hip replacements. We're kind of brothers in that regard. We kind of kid each other about setting alarms off together."
-- Duke basketball coach Mike Krzyzewski

"Most of us would settle for the kind of inscription that could easily be his epitaph: "Here lies the nicest, kindest man you could hope to meet. ... and a darn good sportswriter."
-- East Carolina athletics director Terry Holland

CREDITS:

Chip Alexander— The News & Observer
David Cutcliffe — The News & Observer
Kyle Maynard — The News & Observer, Wikipedia
Rudy Ruettiger— The News & Observer
Kristy Overton — A.J. Carr
Bear Bryant — University of Alabama
Lennie Rosenbluth — UNC athletics
Webb Simpson — PGA Media Guide
Duke — CBS
David Thompson—GoPack.com
Charlie Boswell — Alabama Hall of Fame
Catfish — Brainy Quote website
John Isner — Wikipedia, ATP Media Guide
Rock Marciano — Greensboro Daily News
Mia Hamm — UNC Athletics Dept., Wikipedia, Harper Collins Publishing
Ron Lievense — The News & Observer, Barton College
Dave Odom — Wake Forest Athletics
M.L. Carr — The News & Observer
East Carolina — The News & Observer
George Williams — St. Augustine's College
Jim Ritcher — GoPack.Com, College Football Hall of Fame website
Pat Teague — GoPack.com
Raymond Berry — The News & Observer, NFL statistics
Erik Green — Virginia Tech Athletics Department
Rod Brind' Amour — Carolina Hurricanes website
Tim Duncan – Wikipedia stat
Shane Battier, Steve Wojciechowski –GoDuke.com
Danny Lotz, Albert Long—The News & Observer
Terry Holland – Wikipedia
Simone Biles – blog.gkelite
Vernon Davis – Foxsports, Bill Reiter
Glenn Wesley – M is Good, Dave Jones

Printed in the United States
By Bookmasters